Aprende Inglés con Historias Cortas para Principiantes

[Learn English With Short Stories for Beginners]

15 Historias Cortas para Aprender Inglés Escuchando. ¡Con Vocabularios y Ejercicios!

Escrito por
Learn Like a Native

Tabla de contenido

INTRODUCCIÓN

Aprender un nuevo idioma es un poco como cocinar: necesita varios ingredientes diferentes y la técnica correcta, pero el resultado final seguramente será delicioso. Creamos este libro lleno de historias cortas para aprender español porque el idioma está vivo. El lenguaje se trata de los sentidos: escuchar, saborear las palabras en la lengua y tocar de cerca otra cultura. Aprender un idioma en un aula es un buen lugar para comenzar, pero no es una introducción completa a un idioma.

En este libro, encontrarás un lenguaje que cobra vida. Estas historias cortas son inmersiones en miniatura en el idioma español, a un nivel perfecto para principiantes. Este libro no es una conferencia sobre gramática. No es una lista interminable de vocabulario. Este libro es lo más cercano a una inmersión lingüística sin salir del país. En las historias internas, verá personas que se hablan entre sí, pasan por situaciones de la vida diaria y usan las palabras y frases más comunes y útiles en el lenguaje. Tienes la clave para dar vida a tus estudios de inglés.

5

Hecho para Principiantes

Hicimos este libro con los principiantes en mente. Encontrará que el idioma es simple, pero no aburrido. La mayor parte del libro está en tiempo presente, por lo que podrá centrarse en los diálogos, los verbos raíz y comprender y encontrar patrones en el acuerdo sujeto-verbo.

Esto no es "solo" un libro traducido. Si bien leer novelas e historias cortas traducidas al inglés es algo maravilloso, los principiantes (e incluso los novatos) a menudo se encuentran con dificultades. Las licencias literarias y la estructura compleja de las oraciones pueden hacer que la lectura en su segundo idioma sea realmente difícil, por no mencionar ABURRIDA. Es por eso que *Learn English for Beginners* es el libro perfecto para aprender. Las historias son simples, pero no infantiles. No fueron escritos para niños, pero el lenguaje es simple para que los principiantes puedan aprenderlo.

Los Beneficios de Aprender un Segundo Idioma

Si ha leído este libro, es probable que ya conozca los muchos beneficios de aprender un segundo idioma. Además de ser divertido, saber más de un idioma te abre un mundo completamente nuevo. Podrás comunicarte con una parte mucho más grande del mundo. Se abrirán oportunidades en la fuerza laboral, y tal vez incluso se mejore su trabajo diario. La comunicación mejorada también puede ayudarlo a expandir su negocio. Y desde una perspectiva neurológica, ¡aprender un segundo idioma es como tomar sus vitaminas diarias y comer bien para su cerebro!

Cómo Usar el Libro

Todos los capítulos de este libro siguen la misma estructura:
- Una historia corta.
- Una lista de palabras y frases importantes y relevantes.
- Un resumen en inglés.

- Preguntas para evaluar su comprensión.
- Respuestas para verificar.

Puedes usar este libro, sin embargo, será cómodo para ti, pero tenemos algunas recomendaciones para aprovechar al máximo la experiencia. Pruebe estos consejos y, si funcionan, puede usarlos en cada capítulo del libro.

1. Comience leyendo la historia hasta el final. No te detengas ni te obsesiones con ninguna palabra o frase en particular. Vea cuánto de la trama puede entender de esta manera. Creemos que obtendrá mucho más de lo que puede esperar, pero es completamente normal no entender todo en la historia. Estás aprendiendo un nuevo idioma, y eso lleva tiempo.

2. Lea el resumen en inglés. Vea si coincide con lo que ha entendido de la trama.

3. Lea la historia nuevamente, esta vez más despacio. Vea si puede captar el significado de cualquier palabra o frase que no entienda utilizando pistas de contexto y la información

del resumen. Si hay palabras o frases que no comprende, subráyelas o resáltelas.

4. ¡Ponte a prueba! Trata de responder las cinco preguntas de comprensión que vienen al final de cada historia. Escriba sus respuestas y luego compárelas con las respuestas. ¿Qué tal? Si no los obtuviste todas, ¡no te preocupes!

5. Revise la lista de vocabulario que acompaña al capítulo. ¿Alguna de estas son las palabras que no entendiste? ¿Ya sabías el significado de algunos de ellos por tu lectura?

6. Ahora repase la historia una vez más. Preste atención esta vez a las palabras y frases que ha subrayado o resaltado. Si lo desea, tómese el tiempo de buscarlos para ampliar su significado de la historia. Cada vez que leas la historia, entenderás más y más.

7. Pase al siguiente capítulo cuando esté listo.

Lee y Escucha

Le recomendamos encarecidamente que descargue la versión de audio de este libro. Cuando compra el audiolibro, obtiene la versión .pdf de *"English Stories for Beginners"* de forma gratuita. La versión de audio es la mejor manera de experimentar esto, ya que escuchará a un hablante nativo de inglés contarle cada historia antes o mientras lee. Te irás acostumbrando a su acento a medida que leas, una gran ventaja para cuando quieras aplicar tus nuevas habilidades lingüísticas en el mundo real.

No esperes otro día para comenzar tu viaje para aprender otro idioma. Agregue este libro a su estantería hoy y felicítese por hacer algo para mejorar. ¡Pequeños pasos se suman a grandes avances! Ningún momento es mejor para comenzar a aprender que el presente.

CAPÍTULO 1: El Paquete Misterioso / Saludos - The Mysterious Package / Greetings

The doorbell rings.

Andrew runs to the door of the apartment. The doorbell never rings on Saturday mornings. Andrew is excited to see who is at the door. He opens the door.

"**Good morning**, little boy," says a delivery man. The man is dressed in a brown uniform and is carrying a brown box.

"**Hello, sir**," says Andrew.

"I have a package," the delivery man says. "It says 10 Main Street."

"This is 10 Main Street," says Andrew.

"The package has no name," says the delivery man. "It also has no apartment number."

"How strange!" says Andrew.

"Can you give it to the right person?" the man asks.

"I can try," says Andrew. He is only ten years old, but he feels important.
"Thank you very much," says the delivery man. He leaves. Andrew takes the box into his house. He stares at the box. It is about the size of a shoe box. It has no name on the outside, just 10 Main Street.

Andrew opens the cardboard box. He needs to know what is inside to find the owner. There is a small wood box inside the cardboard box. Andrew opens the wooden box. Inside the box are 10 different pairs of eyeglasses. They are different colors: pink and red, green polka dots, black and white. They are also different shapes: round, square and rectangle.

He closes the box and puts on his shoes.

"**Bye** mom! I'll be right back," he shouts.

Andrew knocks on the door across the hall from his house. It opens. A very old lady smiles at Andrew and the box.

"**Morning**, Mrs. Smith!" says Andrew.

"**How are you?**" asks the old lady.

"**Fine, thanks! And you?**" says Andrew.

"What do you have?" asks the old lady.

"**Ma'am,** this is a package. It belongs to someone in this building but I don't know who," says Andrew.

"It's not for me," says the old lady. "Impossible!"

"Oh, ok" says Andrew, disappointed. The old lady wears glasses. He thinks these glasses would look nice on her. He turns to leave.

"Come back later," calls the old lady. "I'm making cookies and some cookies are for you and your family."

Andrew goes up the stairs. His building has three floors. He is friends with almost everyone in the building. However, the apartment on the second floor has a new family. Andrew doesn't know them. He feels shy, but he rings the bell. A brown-haired man opens the door. He smiles.

"Hi!" says the man.

"Hello," says Andrew. "I live downstairs. **My name is** Andrew."

"It's nice to meet you, Andrew," the man says. "We are new to the building. I'm Mr. Jones."
"Nice to meet you too," says Andrew. "This package belongs to someone in this building. Is it your package?"

"Impossible!" says the man. "My family and I just moved here. No one knows our address."

"Ok," says Andrew. "Nice to meet you then." The door closes. Another no. There are only two apartments left to try. In the next apartment is a family. The daughter goes to the same school as Andrew. She is a year older than Andrew. Her name is Diana. Andrew thinks she is very beautiful. He feels shy again, but he knocks on the door.

A pretty, blonde girl opens the door.

"Hey, Diana," Andrew smiles.

"What's up?" Diana says. Her pijamas are bright pink and her hair is messy.
"How's it going?" Andrew asks.

"It's going," Diana says. "I was asleep. You woke me up."

"I'm sorry," he says quickly. His face is red. He feels extra shy. "I have a package. We don't know who it belongs to."

"What is in it?" asks Diana.

"Some glasses. They are glasses for reading," says Andrew.

"I don't wear glasses. My mom doesn't use them. The box is not for us," says Diana.

"Ok," says Andrew. He waves goodbye and climbs the stairs. There is one more apartment, the apartment on the third floor. Mr. Edwards lives in this apartment, alone. He has a big parrot that knows how to talk. He also has four cats and a dog. His apartment is old and dark. Andrew feels afraid of Mr. Edwards. He rings the doorbell. He has to find out who the box belongs to.

"Hello," says Mr. Edwards. His dog comes to the door. The dog helps Mr. Edwards because he is blind.

"Hi, Mr. Edwards. It's Andrew," Andrew says. Mr. Edwards has his eyes closed. He smiles.

"What's new, Andrew?" He asks. Hmmm, Andrew thinks, maybe Mr. Edwards isn't scary. Maybe Mr. Edwards is just a nice old man that lives alone.

"I have a package and I think it is for you," says Andrew.

"Ah yes! My reading glasses. Finally!" smiles Mr. Edwards. He holds his hands out. Andrew is confused. He looks at the dog. It seems to be smiling, too. He gives Mr. Edwards the box.

"It's good to see you," says Mr. Edwards.

"You too," says Andrew. Maybe he will visit Mr. Edwards another day. He turns around and goes home.

SUMMARY

A boy, Andrew, gets a package not meant for him. It is a box of eyeglasses. He takes it to the neighbors, one by one, to find out who the package belongs to. He finds out the package belongs to his neighbor Mr. Edwards, which is a bit surprising.

Lista de Vocabulario

Good morning	Buenos días
Hello	Hola

Sir	Señor
Thank you very much	Muchas gracias
Bye	Adiós
Morning!	Buen día
How are you?	¿Cómo estás?
Fine, thanks!	¡Bien, gracias!
And you?	¿Y tú? / ¿Y usted?
Ma'am	Señora
Hi	Hola
My name is...	Mi nombre es...
It's nice to meet you	Es un placer conocerte
Nice to meet you too	Encantado de conocerte también
How's it going?	¿Qué tal te va?
It's going	Todo bien

Hey	Hey
What's up	Qué pasa
What's new	Qué hay de nuevo
It's good to see you	Me alegro de verte

QUESTIONS

1. Who is at the front door when Andrew opens it?

    a) a delivery man

    b) a cat

    c) a census taker

    d) his father

2. How would you describe Mrs. Smith?

    a) a beautiful girl

    b) a mean person

    c) a bad neighbor

    d) a kind old woman

3. Who lives on the second floor of the apartment building?

    a) no one

b) a girl from Andrew's school

c) a new family

d) Andrew

4. How do you think Andrew feels about Diana?

a) he likes her and thinks she is pretty

b) he follows her on social media

c) he dislikes her

d) they do not know each other

5. Who in the apartment building do the glasses belong to?

a) the old woman

b) the blind man

c) Andrew and his family

d) no one

ANSWERS

1. Who is at the front door when Andrew opens it?

a) a delivery man

2. How would you describe Mrs. Smith?

d) a kind old woman

3. Who lives on the second floor of the apartment building?

    c) a new family

4. How do you think Andrew feels about Diana?

    a) he likes her and thinks she is pretty

5. Who in the apartment building do the glasses belong to?

    b) the blind man

CAPÍTULO 2: Carnaval / Colores y Días de la Semana - Mardi Gras / Colors + Days of the Week

STORY

Frank steps out his front door. His new house is **violet** with **blue** windows. The **colors** are very bright for a house. In New Orleans, his new home, buildings are colorful.

He is new to the neighborhood. Frank does not have any friends yet. The house next to him is a tall, **red** building. A family lives there. Frank stares at the door, and a man opens it. Frank says hello.

"Hello, neighbor!" says George. He waves. Frank walks to the red house.

"Hi, I'm Frank, the new neighbor," says Frank.

"Nice to meet you. My name is George," George says. The men shake hands. George has a string of lights in his hands. The lights are **green**, **purple** and **gold**.

"What are the lights for?" asks Frank.

"You *are* new," laughs George. "It's Mardi Gras, didn't you know? These colors represent the holiday of carnival here in New Orleans."

"Oh, yes," says Frank. Frank does not know about carnival. He also has no friends to make plans with.

"Today is **Friday**," says George. "There is a parade called Endymion. Will you come with me and the family to watch?"

"Yes," Frank says. "Wonderful!"

George puts the lights on the house. Frank helps George. George turns on the lights. The house looks festive.

The family and Frank go to the parade. During Mardi Gras in New Orleans, there are parades every day. The parades during the **week** are small. The parades on the weekend, **Saturday** and **Sunday**, are big, with many floats and people. There is a king of Mardi Gras. His name is Rex.

Mardi Gras means 'Fat **Tuesday**.' In England, it is called Shrove Tuesday. The holiday is Catholic. It is one day before Ash **Wednesday**, the beginning of Lent. Mardi Gras is the celebration before Lent, a serious time. By **Thursday**, the special days are finished. New Orleans is famous for its Mardi Gras. People have parties and wear masks and costumes. In fact, you can only wear a mask in New Orleans on Mardi Gras. The rest of the year it is illegal!

George and his family watch the parade begin with Frank. Frank is surprised. There are many people watching. They stand in the grass. Floats pass the group. Floats are big structures with people and decorations. They go down the street, one by one.

The first float represents the sun. It has **yellow** decorations. A woman in the middle wears a **white** dress. She looks like an angel. She throws **orange** toys and beads to the people.

"Why does she throw the toys and necklaces?" asks Frank.

"For us!" says Hannah, George's wife. Hannah holds five necklaces in her hands. Some beads are on the ground. Nobody catches them. They are dirty and **brown**.

The parade continues. There are many floats, and many beads. George and his family shout, "Throw me something, mister!" Hannah fills her **black** bag with colorful toys and beads from the floats. Frank learns to shout "Throw me something!" to get beads for himself.

One big float has over 250 people on it. It is the largest in the world.

Finally, the parade ends. The children and the adults are happy. Everyone goes home. Frank is tired. He is also hungry and wants to eat. He follows George and his family into the **red** house. There is a big, round cake on the table. It looks like a ring, with a hole in the middle. The cake has **purple**, **green** and **yellow** frosting on top.

"This is king cake," Hannah says. "We eat king cake every Mardi Gras."

Hannah cuts a piece of cake. She gives one piece to George, one piece to the children, and one piece to Frank. Frank tastes the cake. It is delicious! It tastes like cinnamon. It is soft. But suddenly Frank bites into plastic.

"Ouch!" says Frank. Frank stops eating. He pulls a plastic baby out of the cake.

"There is one more tradition," says George. "The cake has a baby in it. The person who gets the baby buys the next cake."

"That's me!" Frank says.

Everyone laughs. George invites Frank to another parade on **Monday.**

Frank goes home happy. He loves Mardi Gras.

Lista de Vocabulario

violet	violeta
blue	azul
colors	colores
red	rojo
green	verde
purple	púrpura
gold	dorado
Friday	Viernes
week	semana
Saturday	Sábado
Sunday	Domingo

Tuesday	Martes
Wednesday	Miércoles
Thursday	Jueves
yellow	amarillo
white	blanco
orange	naranja
brown	marrón
black	negro
Monday	Lunes

QUESTIONS

1) How would you describe Frank's new house?

    a) boring

    b) colorful

    c) tiny

    d) lonely

2) Which color represents Mardi Gras in New Orleans?

a) blue

b) white

c) orange

d) gold

3) Mardi Gras is a celebration:

    a) for adults only.

    b) from the tradition of the Jewish church.

    c) famous in New Orleans.

    d) you do inside a house.

4) Which of these are not on a Mardi Gras float?

    a) people

    b) computers

    c) toys

    d) beads

5) What happens if you find the baby in a king cake?

    a) you cry

    b) you must take care of the baby

    c) give it to your friend

    d) you must buy a king cake

ANSWERS

1) How would you describe Frank's new house?

    a) boring

2) Which color represents Mardi Gras in New Orleans?

    d) gold

3) Mardi Gras is a celebration:

    c) famous in New Orleans.

4) Which of these are not on a Mardi Gras float?

    b) computers

5) What happens if you find the baby in a king cake?

    d) you must buy a king cake

CAPÍTULO 3: Clima Extraño / Clima - Weird Weather / Weather

STORY

Ivan is twelve years old. He visits his grandparents on the weekend. He loves to visit his grandparents. Grandma gives him cookies and milk every day. Grandpa teaches him neat things. This weekend he goes to their house.

It is February. Where Ivan is, it is **winter**. In February, it usually **snows**. Ivan loves the snow. He plays in it and rolls it into balls. This February weekend, the **weather** is different. The sun is shining; it is **sunny** and almost **hot**! Ivan wears a T-shirt to his grandparent's house.

"Hi, Grandpa! Hi, Grandma!" Ivan says.

"Hello, Ivan!" Grandma says.

"Ivan! How are you?" says Grandpa.

"I'm good," he says, and he hugs his grandparents. Ivan says goodbye to his mom.

They go into the house. "This weather is strange," says Grandma. "February is always **cold** and **cloudy**. I don't understand!"

"It is **climate change**," says Ivan. In school, Ivan learns about contamination and pollution. The weather changes because of changes in the **atmosphere**. Climate change is the difference in the weather over time.

"I don't know about climate change," says Grandpa. "I **predict** the weather by what I see."

"What do you mean?" asks Ivan.

"This morning, the **sky** is red," says Grandpa. "This means I know a **storm** is coming."

"How?" asks Ivan.

"Red sky in the morning, sailors take warning. Red sky at night, sailor's delight." Grandpa tells Ivan about this saying.

If the sky is red at sunrise, it means there is water in the air. The light of the sun shines red. The storm is coming towards you. If the sky is red at sunset, the bad weather is leaving. Without **weathermen**, people watch the sky for clues about the weather.

"How do weathermen predict the weather?" asks Ivan.

"They look at patterns in the atmosphere," says Grandma. "They look at temperature, if it is hot or cold. And they look at air pressure, what is happening in the atmosphere."

"I predict the weather differently," says Grandpa. "For example, I know today it will **rain**."

"How?" asks Ivan.

"The cat," says Grandpa. Ivan looks at the cat. The cat opens its mouth and says 'ah-CHOO'.

"When the cat sneezes or snores, that means rain is coming," says Grandpa. It may **drizzle** or it may be very **rainy**, but it will rain."

Suddenly, they hear a loud sound. Ivan looks out the window. Drops of rain are falling hard. The rain is loud. Ivan can't hear what his Grandpa says.

"What?" says Ivan.

"It's **raining cats and dogs,**" says Grandpa, smiling.

"Ha!" laughs Ivan.

"I know another way to tell the weather," says Grandma.

Grandma watches the spiders to see when the weather will be cold. At the end of **summer**, the weather changes. **Autumn** brings fresh, cool air. Grandma knows that when spiders come inside, it means cold weather is coming. The spiders make a house inside before winter. That is how grandma knows when the winter weather comes.

The rain stops. Grandpa and Ivan go out. Grandpa and Grandma live in a house in the forest. The house has trees around it. It is a small house. Ivan is cold in his T-shirt. The weather is not sunny. The air is moving. It is **windy**. The wind blows through Ivan's hair.

"It is **cold** now," says Ivan.

"Yes," says Grandpa. "What is the temperature?"

"I don't know," says Ivan. "I don't have a thermometer."

"You don't need one," says Grandpa. Grandpa tells Ivan to listen. Ivan hears a sound: *cri-cri-cri*. It is an insect. The *cri-cri-cri* is the sound of crickets. Grandpa teaches Ivan. Ivan counts the *cri* for fourteen seconds. Grandpa adds 40 to that number. That is the temperature outside. Ivan did not know crickets were like thermometers.

Grandma comes out of the house. She smiles. She watches Ivan counting the *cri* sound. "Time for cookies and milk!" she says.

"Yay!" says Ivan.

"Oh, look!" says Grandma. "It's a rainbow." The rainbow goes from the house to the forest. It has many colors: red, orange, yellow, blue and green. The rainbow is beautiful. Grandma, Grandpa and Ivan watch the rainbow. It disappears and they go inside.

"Cookies and milk for everyone," says Grandma. She gives Ivan a warm chocolate cookie.

"Not for me," says Grandpa. "I want tea."

"Why tea?" says Grandma. She has two milks in her hand.

"I'm feeling **under the weather**," says Grandpa. He laughs. Ivan and Grandma laugh with him.

Lista de Vocabulario

winter	invierno
to snow	nevar
weather	clima
sunny	soleado
hot	caliente
cold	frío
cloudy	nublado
climate change	cambio climático
atmosphere	atmosfera
predict	predecir
sky	cielo
storm	tormenta
weathermen	meteorólogo
drizzle	llovizna

rainy	lluvioso
raining cats and dogs	lloviendo gatos y perros
summer	verano
autumn	otoño
windy	ventoso
temperature	temperatura
thermometer	termómetro
rainbow	arcoíris
under the weather	mal tiempo

QUESTIONS

1) What is the weather in February usually like?
   a) hot
   b) cold
   c) sunny
   d) fresh

2) How does Grandpa know what the weather will be like?

    a) he watches television

    b) the weathermen

    c) he observes nature

    d) he does not predict the weather

3) What does it mean to rain cats and dogs?

    a) the rain gets the cats wet

    b) it is raining just a little

    c) cats and dogs fall from the sky

    d) it is raining very hard

4) What does it mean when spiders come inside?

    a) they are hungry

    b) they are ready to lay eggs

    c) cold weather is coming

    d) warm weather is coming

5) Why does Grandpa ask for tea instead of milk?

    a) he feels a bit sick

    b) he is allergic to milk

    c) he wants a hot drink

    d) to make Grandma mad

ANSWERS

1) What is the weather in February usually like?
    a) hot

2) How does Grandpa know what the weather will be like?
    c) he observes nature

3) What does it mean to rain cats and dogs?
    d) it is raining very hard

4) What does it mean when spiders come inside?
    c) cold weather is coming

5) Why does Grandpa ask for tea instead of milk?
    a) he feels a bit sick

CAPÍTULO 4: Deberes de John / Escuela y Aula - John's Homework / School + Classroom

Mrs. Kloss is a grade 4 **teacher**. She teaches at Homewood Elementary School. The **school** is in a red brick building. It is in a small town.

Mrs. Kloss has a **class** of 15 students. Her **students** are boys and girls. They are usually good students. Mrs. Kloss has a routine. Her students start the day at their **desks**, seated in their **chairs**. Mrs. Kloss calls **roll call**.

"Louise?" she says.

"Here!" shouts Louise.

"Mike?" says Mrs. Kloss.

"Present," says Mike.

"John?"

"Here, Mrs. Kloss," John says.

And so on. After roll call, Mrs. Kloss starts the day with **math**. For her students, math is difficult. The class listens to Mrs. Kloss teach. They watch as she writes on the **blackboard**. Sometimes, one student solves a problem in front of the class. They use **chalk** to write out the solution. The other students do the problems in their **notebooks**.

Everyone's favorite time is lunch time. The class goes to the lunchroom. They have two choices. One choice is a healthy meal of meat and vegetables. The other choice is pizza or hamburgers. Some students bring a lunch from home.

In the afternoon, they study **history**. On Fridays, they have **science** class in the **lab**. They do **experiments**, like growing plants from a piece of potato.

Mrs. Kloss gives her students **homework** every day. They take the work home. They work at night. The next day, they bring it to school. The only excuse for incomplete homework is a note from their parents.

One day, the class reviews the **English** homework together.

"Everyone, please bring your **papers** to my desk," says Mrs. Kloss. Everyone brings their homework to Mrs. Kloss. Everyone except for John.

"John, where is your homework?" says Mrs. Kloss.

John's face is very red. He is nervous.

"I don't have it," says John.

"Do you have a note from your parents?" asks Mrs. Kloss.

"No," says John.

"Why didn't you do your homework, then?" asks Mrs. Kloss. John says something very quietly.

"What? We can't hear you," says Mrs. Kloss. She gives John a kind smile. He looks nervous.

"My dog ate my homework," says John. Mrs. Kloss and the other students laugh. This excuse is the most typical excuse for not having work done.

"Is it in your **backpack**? Or maybe your **locker**?" asks Mrs. Kloss. She wants to help John.

"No, my dog ate it!" insists John.

"That's the **oldest excuse in the book**," says Mrs. Kloss.

"It is true!" says John. John is a good student. He usually makes **straight A's**. Mrs. Kloss does not want to send Jon to the **principal's office** for lying. She does not believe John, but she decides to give him another chance.

"Bring the homework tomorrow," says Mrs. Kloss. "Here is another copy." John takes the **worksheet** and thanks Mrs. Kloss. The class turns to their **art** notebook. Today in art class they are drawing a picture with colored **pencils**. Students love art class. It is a chance to relax. They draw and draw until the **bell** rings. School is over.

Students talk in the hallways. They exchange notes. The Grade 4 students wait outside. Their parents pick them up. Some of them are on foot. Some of them are in cars. The teachers help them to find their parents.

Mrs. Kloss finishes her work. She packs her **laptop** into her bag. Her classroom is clean and empty. She goes outside. As she walks to her car, she see John and his dad. John's father picks him up with their dog. Mrs. Kloss waves to John and his father.

"Hello, John!" says Mrs. Kloss.

"Good afternoon, Mrs. Kloss," John says.

"Is this the dog that ate your homework?" asks Mrs. Kloss. She smiles, so John knows she is teasing.

"Yes, Mrs. Kloss," says John's father. "Thank you for understanding. John is so worried about getting in trouble!"
Mrs. Kloss is shocked! This time, the dog really did eat the homework.

Lista de Vocabulario

teacher	profesor / profesora
school	escuela
class	clase
students	estudiantes
desk	escritorio
chair	silla
roll call	pasar lista
math	matemáticas
blackboard	pizarra

chalk	tiza
notebook	cuaderno
history	historia
science	ciencia
lab	laboratorio
experiment	experimento
homework	tarea
English	inglés
papers	papeles
backpack	mochila
locker	casillero
the oldest excuse in the book	la excusa más antigua del libro
straight A's	sobresaliente
principal's office	oficina del director

worksheet	hoja de trabajo
pencils	lápices
bell	campana
laptop	laptop

QUESTIONS

1) How does the day begin in Mrs. Kloss's class?

    a) the students stand and shout

    b) with a homework assignment

    c) roll call

    d) Mrs. Kloss shouts

2) What is everyone's favorite time of day at Homewood Elementary School?

    a) roll call

    b) lunch time

    c) math class

    d) after the bell rings

3) Why does Mrs. Kloss say that John's excuse is the oldest in the book?

    a) because everyone uses that excuse

b) John is the oldest in the class

c) he forgot his book

d) his dog is seven years old

4) What do you have to have if you don't do your homework?

a) a science experiment

b) a good excuse

c) nothing, it's fine

d) a note from your parents

5) Why is Mrs. Kloss surprised at the end of the story?

a) she realizes John was telling the truth

b) John's dog is actually a horse

c) John does not speak to her

d) John's dad looks just like John

ANSWERS

1) How does the day begin in Mrs. Kloss's class?

c) roll call

2) What is everyone's favorite time of day at Homewood Elementary School?

b) lunch time

3) Why does Mrs. Kloss say that John's excuse is the oldest in the book?

    a) because everyone uses that excuse

4) What do you have to have if you don't do your homework?

    d) a note from your parents

5) Why is Mrs. Kloss surprised at the end of the story?

    a) she realizes John was telling the truth

CAPÍTULO 5: Oferta de Tienda de Segunda Mano / Casa y Muebles - Thrift Store Bargain / house and furniture

STORY

Louise and Mary are best friends. They are also **roommates**. They share an **apartment** in the center of town. Today they want to shop for **furniture** for their **home**. Louise and Mary are both students. They do not have much money.

"Where can we shop?" Louise asks Mary.

"We need a lot of furniture," Mary says. She is worried about money.

"I know," says Louise. "We need to find a **bargain**."

"I have an idea. Let's go to the thrift store!" says Mary.

"Great idea!" says Louise.

The two girls drive the car to the thrift store. It is a giant store. The building is bigger than ten **houses**.

The girls park the car. The parking lot is empty.

"Wow," says Louise. "The store is very big."

"Totally," says Mary. "And there is nobody here."

"We will be the only people," says Louise. "We can **make ourselves at home.**"

The girls walk into the store. The store has everything. On the right, there is the **kitchen** section. There are tall **refrigerators** and old **microwaves** on the **shelves**. There are **toasters** of all colors. The prices are good. A microwave costs only $10.

Everything is a bargain. The items are used and second-hand. However, Mary and Louise find items that they like. There are more than a dozen sofas. Mary and Louise need a **sofa**. They spend time talking about the different sofas. Mary likes a brown leather sofa. Louise likes a big purple sofa. They cannot decide. Louise sees a purple **chair**. The girls decide to get the purple sofa and chair so that they match. It is perfect for their home.

"I need a **bed** for my **bedroom**," says Louise.

The girls walk to the bedroom area. First, they pass the art section.

"You know, we need something for the **walls**," says Louise. Mary agrees. There are big paintings, small paintings, empty **frames**, and photographs in frames. Louise decides on a big, abstract painting. It has lines of splattered red, blue, and black paint.

"I can paint like that," says Mary. "It looks like a child's painting."

"It's only five dollars," says Louise.

"Oh, ok!" says Mary.

The girls finish shopping. Louise also finds a **lamp** for her bedroom. Her bedroom is too dark. Mary chooses a **carpet** for the **bathroom**. The girls are very happy. They spend only $100 dollars for all the furniture.

"That is why shopping at the thrift store is a bargain," says Louise.

"Yes, we got **everything but the kitchen sink**!" says Mary.

Mary and Louise have a party in their apartment that night. It is a party to welcome friends. Mary and Louise want to show their new furniture.

The doorbell rings. Mary opens the **door**. Nick is the first to arrive. Nick is Mary's friend. Nick is also a student. He studies art history.

"Hi, ladies," says Nick. "Thank you for inviting me."

"Come in, Nick!" says Mary. Nick steps into the **foyer**. She hugs him.

"Do you want to see our new stuff?" asks Louise.

"Yeah!" says Nick.

Louise and Mary show Nick around the apartment. They are happy with the **living room**. The new sofa, chair and painting looks great.

"All of this is from the thrift store," says Mary. She is proud.

Nick walks up to the painting. "I really like this painting," he says.

"I do too," says Louise. "I chose it."

"It reminds me of Jackson Pollock," says Nick.

"Who is Jackson Pollock?" asks Mary.

"He is a very famous painter," says Nick. "He splashes paint onto canvas. Just like this one." Nick looks closely at the painting.

"Is it signed?" he asks. Louise shakes her head no. "Let's look behind it then."

They take the painting out of the frame and turn it around. They all are quiet. On the bottom is a signature that looks like 'Jackson Pollock'.

"How much did you pay for this?" asks Nick.

"About five dollars," says Louise.

"This is probably worth at least $10 million dollars," says Nick. He is shocked. Mary looks at Louise. Louise looks at Mary.

"Does anyone want a glass of champagne?" says Mary.

Now that is a bargain!

Lista de Vocabulario

roommates	compañeros de cuarto
apartment	apartamento

furniture	mueble
home	hogar
bargain	Oferta / Ganga
thrift store	tienda de segunda mano
house	casa
make ourselves at home	sentirnos como en casa
kitchen	cocina
refrigerators	refrigeradores
microwaves	microondas
shelves	estantes
toasters	tostadoras
chair	silla
table	mesa
sofa	sofá
bed	cama

bedroom	dormitorio
wall	pared
frame	marco
lamp	lámpara
carpet	alfombra
bathroom	baño
everything but the kitchen sink	todo menos el fregadero de la cocina
door	puerta
foyer	vestíbulo
living room	sala de estar

QUESTIONS

1) Why do Mary and Louise go to the thrift store?

a) They need money.

b) They need furniture but don't have much money.

c) They have furniture to sell.

d) They want to have fun.

2) Why are prices at the thrift store so low?

    a) It is sale season.

    b) It is closing.

    c) The items are used.

    d) The prices are normal, not low.

3) Which of the following items goes in a kitchen?

    a) bed

    b) microwave

    c) shower

    d) sofa

4) How does Nick know so much about the painting?

    a) He is a professional art dealer.

    b) The painting belongs to Nick.

    c) He studies art.

    d) He read a book.

5) At the end, Mary and Louise are...

    a) sad.

    b) surprised and rich.

    c) angry at Nick.

d) too tired to have a party.

ANSWERS

1) Why do Mary and Louise go to the thrift store?

    b) They need furniture but don't have much money.

2) Why are prices at the thrift store so low?

    c) The items are used.

3) Which of the following items goes in a kitchen?

    b) microwave

4) How does Nick know so much about the painting?

    c) He studies art.

5) At the end, Mary and Louise are...

    b) surprised and rich.

CAPÍTULO 6: La Cabra / Verbos Comunes en Tiempo Presente - The Goat / common present tense verbs

Ollie wakes up. The sun is shining. He remembers: it is Saturday. Today his dad does not **work**. That means Ollie and his dad **do** something together. What can they do? Ollie **wants** to go to the movies. He also wants to play video games.

Ollie is twelve years old. He goes to school. Saturday he does not go to school. He **uses** Saturday to do what he wants. His dad lets him decide. So Ollie wants to do something fun.

"Daaaaaad!" **calls** Ollie. "**Come** here!"

Ollie waits.

His dad enters Ollie's bedroom.

"Today is Saturday," **says** Ollie.

"I **know**, son," says Ollie's dad.

"I want to do something fun!" says Ollie.

"Me too," says Dad.

"What can we do?" **asks** Ollie.

"What do you want to do?" asks his dad.

"Go to the movies," says Ollie.

"We always go to the movies on Saturday," says Ollie's dad.

"Play video games," says Ollie.

"We play video games everyday!" says Dad.

"Ok, ok," says Ollie. He **thinks**. He remembers his teacher at school. His teacher **tells** the students to go outside. The teacher tells them the fresh air is good. At school, they study animals. Ollie learns about animals in the jungle, animals in the ocean, and animals on farms.

That's it!

"Dad, let's go to a farm!" says Ollie. Ollie's dad thinks that is a great idea. He has always wanted to **see** and touch farm animals.

They take the car. Ollie's dad drives to the countryside. They see a sign that says "Animal Farm". They follow the signs and park the car.

Ollie and his dad buy tickets to enter. Tickets cost $5. They leave the ticket office. There is a big wooden building, the farmhouse. Behind the farmhouse, there is a huge field. The field has trees, grass, and fences. In each fence is a different type of animal. There are hundreds of animals.

Ollie is excited. He sees chickens, horses, ducks, and pigs. He touches them and listens to them. Ollie **makes** a sound to each animal. To the ducks, he says "quack". To the pigs, he says "oink". To the horses, he says "nay". To the chickens, he says "bok bok". The animals stare at Ollie.

Past the animals in cages, Ollie sees a flock of sheep. Ollie's dad tells him that female sheep are called ewes. Male sheep are rams. Baby sheep are called lambs. The sheep are eating grass.
"They can see us," says Dad.

"But they are not looking at us," says Ollie.

"Sheep can see behind themselves. They don't have to turn their heads," says Dad. Ollie's dad knows a lot about sheep.

"They cut the hair on the sheep in spring," says Dad. He tells Ollie how the sheep's wool **becomes** sweaters, scarves and other warm clothing. Ollie has a sweater made of wool. It is warm.

Ollie and his dad walk around the field. The grass is green. There are cows in a corner. One of the mother cows feeds a baby calf.

"You know what cows make, Ollie?" asks Dad.

"Duh! Milk!" says Ollie.

"That's right," says Dad.

Ollie hears an animal sound. He **takes** his dad's hand. They walk towards the sound. They come to a fence. They **find** a goat. The goat has horns stuck in the fence. The goat sits on the ground. It does not move. Its horns are between the wood and it can't move. Ollie and his dad **look** at the goat.

"I feel so bad for the goat," says Ollie. She seems sad.

"Poor guy!" says Dad.

"He looks so sad," says Ollie.

"We can help him," Dad says.

"Yeah!" says Ollie.

They get close to the goat. Ollie is nervous. Dad says not to worry. The horns are stuck and the goat will not hurt them. Ollie looks into the eyes of the goat. The goat **needs** help. Ollie talks to the goat. He **tries** to make soft sounds. He wants to keep the goat calm.

Ollie's dad tries to move the horns. He tries the right horn. He tries the left horn. They don't move. After ten minutes, they **give up**.

"I can't do it," says Ollie's dad.

"Are you sure?" asks Ollie.

"The horns are stuck," says Dad.

"What do we do?" asks Ollie.

The area around the goat is mud. There is no grass left. Ollie's dad takes some grass from the ground and brings it to the goat. The goat eats the grass. The goat looks hungry. The grass is gone. Ollie gets more grass to take to the goat. They pet the goat for a few minutes. The goat seems grateful.

"Let's tell the owner," says Dad.

"Yeah," says Ollie. "Maybe they can help her."

Ollie and his dad go to the ticket office. The ticket office is a small building at the entrance. A man works there. Ollie and his dad go inside.

"Hello, sir," says Ollie's dad.

"How can I help you?" asks the man.

"There's a goat—" says Ollie's dad.

The man interrupts Ollie's dad. He waves his hand. He looks bored. "Yeah, we know."

"You know about the goat?" asks Ollie.

"The goat stuck in the fence?" asks the man.

"Yes!" say Ollie and his dad.

"Oh yes, that's Patty," says the man. "She can get herself out whenever she wants. She just likes the attention."

Ollie **gives** his dad a surprised look. Ollie and his dad laugh.

"Patty, what a goat!" Ollie says.

SUMMARY

Ollie wakes up on a Saturday. He and his dad decide to do something fun. They go to a farm to see animals. They see and touch many animals: cows, horses, sheep, and more. They walk around the farm. It is a beautiful day. They find a goat trapped in a fence. They try to help the goat. The goat is stuck by the horns. They feed it grass. Ollie and his dad go get help. The man in the ticket office listens to them. He tells them the goat likes to trick people to get attention. Ollie and his dad laugh.

Lista de Vocabulario

to work	trabajar
to do	hacer

to want	querer
to go	ir
to use	utilizar
to call	llamar
to come	venir
to say	decir
to know	saber
to ask	preguntar
to think	pensar
to tell	decir
to see	ver
to become	convertir
to make	hacer
to take	tomar
to find	encontrar

to feel	sentir
to look	mirar
to get	obtener
to need	necesitar
to try	intentar
to give	dar

QUESTIONS

1) What do Ollie and his dad decide to do on Saturday?

    a) go to the movies

    b) go to a farm

    c) play video games

    d) go to school

2) Which animal does Ollie's dad know a lot about?

    a) sheep

    b) pigs

    c) giraffe

    d) cow

3) What is happening to the goat?

a) it hides

b) it eats

c) it is stuck

d) it is angry

4) What do Ollie and his dad do for the goat?

a) free it

b) give it grass and pet it

c) call the police to get it

d) kiss it

5) What does Patty do?

a) she leaves the farm

b) she eats trash

c) she goes to the ticket office

d) acts stuck to get attention

ANSWERS

1) What do Ollie and his dad decide to do on Saturday?

b) go to a farm

2) Which animal does Ollie's dad know a lot about?

a) sheep

3) What is happening to the goat?
    c) it is stuck

4) What do Ollie and his dad do for the goat?
    b) give it grass and pet it

5) What does Patty do?
    d) acts stuck to get attention

CAPÍTULO 7: El Coche / Emociones - The Car / emotions

STORY

Quentin is **interested** in cars. He looks at pictures of cars. He reads about cars all night, every night. When he is **bored**, he scrolls through Instagram. The accounts he follows are all about cars.

Quentin's girlfriend is Rashel. Rashel is **amused** by Quentin's obsession. Cars do not interest her.

Quentin has a car. Quentin drives a 2000 Honda Accord. His car is green. Quentin feels **embarrassed** by his car. He wants a cool car. He wants a car to drive around town with Rashel. He dreams of nice cars, expensive cars. He wants a big car. Small cars are boring.

Lately, Quentin looks at his phone all the time. When Rashel looks at it, Quentin hides the phone.

"Quentin, why do you hide the phone from me?" asks Rashel.

"No reason," says Quentin.

"That's not true!" says Rashel.

"I promise it is!" says Quentin.

"Then let me see the screen," says Rashel.

"It's nothing," says Quentin. "Forget about it."

Rashel is **suspicious**. Quentin is hiding something.

One night, Rashel makes dinner. Quentin's phone rings. She does not know the number. Quentin answers the phone.

"Hello? Oh. I will call you later," says Quentin. He hangs up.

"Who is it?" says Rashel.

"Nobody," says Quentin.

"Is it a girl?" asks Rashel. She is **jealous**.

"No it is not," says Quentin.

"Then who is it?" asks Rashel.
"Nobody," says Quentin.

"Why won't you tell me?" asks Rashel.

He is so **angry**; Quentin walks out of the house. He leaves the food on the table. It gets cold. Rashel is **sad**. The dinner is a waste. Rashel calls her friend. They talk about the dinner. Rashel's friend thinks Quentin is with another girl. Rashel is unsure. Quentin is hiding something. She is sure.

Quentin sits in his car. He opens his laptop. He searches adverts for second-hand cars. There are cheap cars and expensive cars. He is **hopeful**. He looks for a car that is a good bargain. He has a little money. He and

Rashel save money. They use it for vacation. This year, Quentin wants a car, not a vacation.

He sees an advert about an old car. The car is from the year 1990. The car is a Jeep. The model is a Grand Wagoneer. He is **curious** about the car. No cars look like this car. It has wood on the outside. Quentin thinks that is cool.

Quentin calls the number on the advert.

"Hello," says a man.

"Hello," says Quentin. "I am calling about the car."

"Which car?" asks the man.

"The Jeep," says Quentin. "I'll take it."

"Ok," says the man.

"I'll come get it tomorrow," says Quentin.

"Ok!" says the man. He hangs up the phone.

Quentin goes back to the house. He feels **guilty**.
Dinner is cold. He eats it anyway. He is **nervous**. What
will Rashel think about the car?

The next day, Quentin gets the car. Quentin loves the
new car. His car is a 1990 Jeep Grand Wagoneer. It is a
big car. It has wood panels along the side.

Quentin drives to the house. The car has 120,000
kilometers. It is about 30 years old. The car is in very
good condition. Everything works. The interior is like
new. Quentin's new car is special. He does not feel
ashamed driving. On the contrary, he feels **proud**
driving through town. What is not to love?

He knocks on the door. Rashel opens it.

"Rashel," he says. "Look!" Quentin points at the car.

"You have a new car?" she asks.

"Yes," says Quentin. He invites Rashel to ride. The two
drive around town. Quentin drives slow. Many people

stare at the car. It is a special car. Several men look **envious**. They want a cool car. Quentin is finally **happy**.

Quentin spends every day with the Jeep. He drives it. Sometimes he has nowhere to go. He just drives around town. He loves the car. He feels **confident** in the Jeep. He spends every evening cleaning the car. He polishes the doors and windows every night. Rashel waits for him. He is late for dinner. This makes Rashel **enraged**. She hates the Jeep Wagoneer. She thinks Quentin loves the car more than he loves her. She tells Quentin this and he tells her not to be **stupid**. He gives her a **loving** hug. He wants to show her she is wrong.

On Saturday, Rashel and Quentin go to the supermarket. Quentin drives them. The windows are down. Quentin wears sunglasses. He looks **confident** and sure of himself. He parks the car. The two go into the supermarket.

They shop for fruit.

"Quentin, can you get four apples?" asks Rashel. Quentin goes to get the fruit. He returns. But he has four oranges.

"Quentin, I said apples!" says Rashel.

"Yeah, I know," says Quentin.

"These are oranges!" says Rashel.

"Oh, sorry," says Quentin. He is **distracted**. He cannot concentrate.

"What is wrong?" asks Rashel.

"Nothing," says Quentin.

"What are you thinking about?" she asks.

"Nothing," says Quentin. He has an **anxious** look. He has a **worried** look in his eyes.

"Are you thinking about the car?" asks Rashel.

"No," says Quentin.

"Yes you are! I know it! Go get me some apples," says Rashel. She is **determined** to make Quentin pay attention. Quentin brings back the apples. He puts them in the cart.   They finish grocery shopping. Quentin is quiet. He seems **withdrawn**. They go to the car.

The parking lot is full. Quentin inspects the Jeep carefully. He is **afraid** of marks or scratches. A car door leaves marks when it hits another door. There are many cars now. He does not see any scratches. Quentin unlocks the car. He gets in.
Rashel puts the groceries in the car. She returns the cart to the store. She opens the door and gets in.

"Quentin, I am **miserable**," she says. She is crying.

"What?" says Quentin. He is **surprised**. What is wrong?

"You only care about the car," says Rashel.

"That's not true," says Quentin.

"You don't help me do anything," says Rashel.

"I do! I care about you," says Quentin.

"If you care about me, sell this car," says Rashel.

SUMMARY

Quentin wants a new car. He hides his search from his girlfriend Rashel. She asks him who calls. She asks him what he is looking at. But Quentin keeps his search a secret. Quentin finds a car he loves. He is finally happy. However, he is too obsessed with the car. Rashel becomes jealous. Quentin cannot concentrate at the grocery store. He is worried someone will scratch the car. Quentin does not help Rashel with the shopping. She becomes angry. She tells Quentin he must choose between her and the car.

Lista de Vocabulario

| interested | interesado |
| bored | aburrido |

amused	entretenido
suspicious	suspicaz
embarrassed	avergonzado
jealous	celoso
angry	enojado
sad	triste
hopeful	esperanzado
curious	curioso
guilty	culpable
nervous	nervioso
ashamed	avergonzado
proud	orgulloso
envious	envidioso
happy	feliz
enraged	enfurecido

stupid	estúpido
loving	cariñoso
confident	confiado
distracted	distraído
anxious	ansioso
worried	preocupado
determined	determinado
withdrawn	retraido
miserable	miserable
surprised	sorprendido

QUESTIONS

1) What does Quentin think about his car at the beginning of the story?

    a) he loves it

    b) he is embarrassed by it

    c) it is too new

d) it is too expensive

2) Why does Rashel get angry at dinner?

    a) she thinks a girl is calling Quentin

    b) she is hungry

    c) Quentin is late

    d) Quentin forgot to buy bread

3) What does Quentin do at the grocery store?

    a) he pays for everything

    b) he gets oranges instead of apples

    c) he spills milk

    d) he pays attention to Rashel

4) What does Quentin think about his new car?

    a) it is too new

    b) it is too small

    c) he is proud of it

    d) he is embarrassed by it

5) At the end of the story, Quentin and Rashel:

    a) kiss

    b) make up from the fight

    c) leave the store

    d) have a fight

ANSWERS

1) What does Quentin think about his car at the beginning of the story?
    b) he is embarrassed by it

2) Why does Rashel get angry at dinner?
    a) she thinks a girl is calling Quentin

3) What does Quentin do at the grocery store?
    b) he gets oranges instead of apples

4) What does Quentin think about his new car?
    c) he is proud of it

5) At the end of the story, Quentin and Rashel:
    d) have a fight

CAPÍTULO 8 : Ir a una Reunión / Decir la Hora - Going to A Meeting / telling time

STORY

Thomas leaves his apartment building. It is a beautiful day. The sun shines. The air is fresh. Thomas has an important meeting today. Thomas is the CEO of a company. Today he meets with new investors. He is prepared for the meeting. He feels relaxed.

It is **eight o'clock in the morning**. Thomas walks down the city street. He is early. He wants extra **time**. He does not want to be late. He does not want to stress.

Thomas lives in a big city. There are tall buildings everywhere. Taxis drive by. Lots of cars drive by. Thomas likes to walk. Sometimes he takes the subway.

Thomas wants to eat breakfast. He stops at a café. The café is relaxed. Music plays. Thomas wants a baked good.

"What would you like?" asks the barista.

"A muffin please," says Thomas.

"Blueberry or chocolate?" asks the barista.

"Blueberry, please," says Thomas.

"Anything to drink?" asks the barista.

"A coffee," says Thomas.

"Black?" asks the barista.

"No, with a bit of cream," he says.

"To go?" asks the barista. Thomas looks at his watch. It is **half past eight.** He has time.

"For here," says Thomas. He sits down and eats. He watches people walk by. Thomas looks at his watch again. It is nine o'clock **on the dot**. He gets up. Thomas throws out the trash and goes to the bathroom. He takes off his watch to wash his hands. His watch is gold and he doesn't like to get it wet. His phone rings.

"Hello," says Thomas.

"Sir, are you at the office?" asks Thomas's secretary.

"Not yet," says Thomas. "I'm on my way."

He leaves the coffee shop. Thomas walks towards the subway. He has time, so he doesn't need a taxi. He looks at his watch again. But his watch is not there. Thomas feels panic. He thinks back over the morning. Did he leave it at home? No. He remembers taking off the watch and washing his hands. The watch is at the coffee shop.

Thomas runs back to the coffee shop.

"Excuse me," he says to the barista.

"Do you have a gold watch?" he asks.

"Just a **second**," says the barista. He asks his colleagues. No one has the watch.

"No," says the barista. Thomas goes to the bathroom. He looks by the sink. The watch is not there. Someone has the watch, Thomas thinks. He has no time to look any more.

"Excuse me," he says to the barista again.

"**What time is it?**" he asks.

"**Ten oh nine a.m.**" says the barista.

"Thanks," says Thomas. Thomas hurries. He has the meeting at a quarter to eleven. He rushes to the subway stop. There is a long line to buy tickets. He waits for five **minutes**.

"Do you have the time?" Thomas asks a woman.

"It's ten **thirty**," she says. Thomas is late. He leave the long line. He goes to the street. He waves for a taxi. All the taxis are full. Finally, a taxi stops. Thomas gets into the taxi.

"Where are you going?" asks the driver.

"To 116th and Park," says Thomas.

"Ok," says the driver.

"Please hurry," says Thomas. "I need to be **on time** for a meeting."

"Yes, sir," says the driver.

Thomas arrives to the office. He runs out of the taxi and up the stairs. His secretary says hello. Thomas is sweaty!

"Sir, the meeting is now **in an hour**," says the secretary. Thomas wipes the sweat off his face.

"Good," says Thomas. He prepares for the meeting. His shirt is sweaty. It smells bad. Thomas decides to buy a new shirt for the meeting.

Thomas goes to the store down the street.

"Hi, sir," says the salesperson. "How can we help you?"

"I need a new dress shirt," says Thomas. The salesperson takes Thomas to see the shirts. There are pink shirts, brown shirts, checked shirts, and plaid shirts. The salesperson talks a lot. Thomas is nervous about the time.

"**What's the time?**" Thomas asks the salesperson.

"It's **nearly noon**," says the salesperson.

"Ok," says Thomas. "Give me the brown shirt." The salesperson takes the brown shirt to the cash register. She folds the shirt. She **takes her time**.

Thomas's phone rings. It is his wife.

"Honey, we have dinner at seven **p.m.**," she says.

"Ok, dear," says Thomas. "I can't really talk right now."

"Ok," she says. "I just don't want you to come home at nine o'clock **at night**."

"Don't worry," says Thomas.

"Bye," says his wife. Thomas hangs up the phone.

"Excuse me," says Thomas. "I'm in a hurry. I don't need the shirt wrapped."

"Ok," she says. Thomas pays and leaves the store. He changes his shirt as he walks down the street. People stare. He hurries to the office.

"It's **about time**," says his secretary when he walks in. They are waiting in the meeting. The investors sit around the table. Thomas says hello.

"I like your shirt, Thomas," says one of the investors.

"Thanks," says Thomas. "It is new." Thomas sets his phone down and turns on his computer.

"Thank you for coming," says Thomas. "I have a presentation. It is about fifteen minutes long."

Thomas turns to his secretary. "What time is it?"

"It is **twelve fifteen**," she says.

"Thanks," says Thomas. "My watch is missing."

"Why don't you look at your phone for the time?" says one of the investors.

"Of course," says Thomas. He is so accustomed to his watch that he forgets he can look at the phone for the time!

"I must be the last person in the world to only use a watch to **tell the time**," says Thomas. Everyone laughs.

SUMMARY

Thomas begins his day with plenty of time. He eats breakfast and relaxes. He goes to the bathroom and leaves his watch in the bathroom. When he realizes, he goes back to the coffee shop. The watch is gone. Now he must ask everyone what time it is. He arrives late to the office. Fortunately, his meeting is postponed one hour. He goes to buy a new shirt. That takes longer than he expects. He rushes to the meeting. When he asks for the time, again, he realizes he could just look at his phone for the time. The meeting begins.

Lista de Vocabulario

It is ____ o'clock	Son las ____ en punto
in the morning	por la mañana
time	tiempo
half past ____	____ y media
on the dot	en punto
second	segundo
What time is it?	¿Y qué hora es?

oh	y
a.m.	a.m.
a quarter to	un cuarto para las
minutes	minutos
Do you have the time?	¿Tienes la hora?
thirty	y treinta
on time	a tiempo
in an hour	en una hora
What's the time?	¿Cuál es la hora?
nearly	temprano
noon	mediodía
takes her time	tomar su tiempo
p.m.	p.m.
at night	de la noche
about time	sobre el tiempo

minutes long	minutos de largo
fifteen	y quince
tell the time	decir la hora

QUESTIONS

1) Why does Thomas lose his watch?

  a) It falls off

  b) He lets a stranger hold it

  c) He makes a bet

  d) He takes it off to wash his hands

2) Where does Thomas live?

  a) in a small town

  b) in a city with little transportation

  c) in a big city

  d) in the countryside

3) Thomas is lucky because:

  a) he has nice coworkers

  b) his meeting is postponed

  c) the subway is not busy

d) he does not lose his watch

4) Thomas tells the salesperson not to wrap the shirt because:

    a) he is late for his meeting

    b) the sweat on his shirt is showing

    c) his wife waits on the phone

    d) he hates wasting bags

5) Everyone laughs at the end of the story because:

    a) Thomas's shirt is sweaty

    b) Thomas is embarrassed

    c) Thomas forgets you can tell the time on your phone

    d) Thomas loses his watch.

ANSWERS

1) Why does Thomas lose his watch?

    d) He takes it off to wash his hands

2) Where does Thomas live?

    c) in a big city

3) Thomas is lucky because:

      b) his meeting is postponed

4) Thomas tells the salesperson not to wrap the shirt because:

      a) he is late for his meeting

5) Everyone laughs at the end of the story because:

      c) Thomas forgets you can tell the time on your phone

CAPÍTULO 9: Almuerzo con la Reina / Verbo Ser-Estar, Tener y Comida - Lunch With The Queen / to be, to have + food

STORY

Ursula **is** a young girl. She lives in London, England. She studies at school. She loves to bake. She **has** an obsession: the royal family. She wants **to be** a princess.

One night, Ursula is at home. Her mother prepares her dinner. They **have** something new. Her mother brings the plate to the table.

"What **are** those?" asks Ursula.

"These are **leeks**," says Ursula's mom.

"Oh, I don't like leeks," says Ursula.

"Try them," says her mom. She tries them. She almost vomits.

"I **am** sick," says Ursula.

"No, you are not," says her mom.

"Please, give me any other **vegetable**," says Ursula. **"Carrots, broccoli, salad**?"
"Oh, Ursula, just eat your **meat** then," says her mom. She turns on the television. They watch the news. The report is about the Queen of England. Ursula stops eating. She pays close attention.

"Queen Elizabeth reigns in England for 68 years," says the news report. "She is married to Prince Phillip. They have four children."

The news report talks about the Queen. She lives in Buckingham Palace. She is very healthy, despite her age.

"I want to visit Buckingham Palace," says Ursula.

"Yes, dear," says her mom. They watch the program. The program announces a special competition. One person can win a visit to Buckingham Palace. The winner will eat **lunch** with the queen. Ursula screams.

"I **have to** win!" she shouts.

"I don't know," says her mom. "Many people enter the contest."

Ursula watches the program. She learns how to enter. She takes a picture of herself eating. Then she posts it on social media. She watches the program, which talks about eating with the Queen. She watches as they show what happened to a prince from the South Pacific.

The Queen is on a boat with the prince. They serve **dessert**. The prince forgets to watch the Queen. He takes some **grapes** and some **cherries** from the **fruit** on the table and puts them in his bowl. He pours **cream** over them. He sprinkles **sugar** on top. He starts to eat, and then he realizes the Queen has not. He makes a big mistake. The Queen takes her spoon. She eats a bit. That makes the prince feel better. He is very embarrassed.

"There are rules to eat with the Queen?" she asks her mom.

"Of course," says her mom.

"Like what?" asks Ursula.

"Well, the Queen begins the **meal** and ends the meal," says Ursula's mom.

"You mean you can't eat until she does," says Ursula.

"That's right," says her mom. "And when she finishes, you finish, too."

"What if you aren't finished?" asks Ursula.

"You are," says her mom. "And you must wait for the Queen to sit."

"Before you sit?" says Ursula.

"Right," says her mom. Ursula thinks about this. There are lots of rules if you are queen or princess. Ursula and her mom finish dinner. They go to sleep.

The next morning, Ursula wakes up. She is nervous about the contest. Today they announce the winner. She eats **breakfast** with her mom.

"I am nervous," she says.

"Ursula, you won't win," says her mom. "So many people are in the contest."

"Oh," says Ursula. She is sad. She eats her **cereal**. She is not hungry. Her **bacon** and **eggs** sit untouched.

They turn on the television.

"And we announce the winner of the Lunch with the Queen Contest," says the man on the TV. He puts his hand into a huge glass bowl full of papers. He moves his hand around. He pulls out a paper. He opens the paper.

"And the winner is...Ursula Vann!" he says.

Ursula looks at her mom. Her mom looks at her.

"Did you hear that?" she asks. Her mom nods, staring. Her mouth is open.

"Did I win?" she asks. Her mom nods, speechless.

"Woo-hoo!" shouts Ursula. "I knew I would! I'm going to see the queen!" Ursula finishes her food and goes to school.

The next day is the day for lunch with the Queen. Ursula walks up to the palace. She is terrified. She is only a young girl. This is a big adventure for such a young girl.

"Who are you?" asks a guard.

"Ursula Vann," she says. "I won the contest to have lunch with the Queen."

"Oh, hello, young lady," the guard says. "You are a pretty young lass. Come in."

"Thank you," she says.

A guard takes her to the palace. It is grand, and very big. They walk through the halls. The guard has a funny hat. Ursula giggles. Then, she stops. They are in the dining room.

The Queen of England is sitting at the table! There is a plate of **sandwiches** in front of her. She is small. She is happy, and she is smiling.

"Hello, dear," she says.

"Hello, your majesty," Ursula says. She courtsies.

"Thank you for coming to lunch," she says.

"It is my pleasure, your **Majesty**," says Ursula.

"I hope you don't mind. We will be having **tea** instead of a proper lunch," says the Queen. She sits again. Ursula remembers her manners. She sits, too.

The sandwiches are royal sandwiches, she thinks. They look a lot like sandwiches from home, though. Some have **ham** and **cheese**, with a yellow bit of **mustard**. Others have a **mayonnaise** salad on them. There is a plate of **cookies** next to some **scones**.

"Pardon me, your Majesty," says Ursula.

"Yes, dear?" says the Queen.

"What is on that sandwich?" she asks.

"Oh, that's my favorite," says the Queen. "Leek **salad** sandwich."

"Oh, leeks," says Ursula. She feels sick. The Queen reaches for one. She takes a bite.

"Have one, dear," says the Queen.

"Thank you, your Majesty," says Ursula. She takes a leek sandwich. She can feel her stomach turn. She takes a huge bite because she is so nervous. Her face turns white, then green.

"Are you alright, dear?" asks the Queen. "You look quite unwell."

"I- I- I'm fine," says Ursula. She feels her stomach turning. She feels as if she will vomit. She can't stop the leeks from coming back up her throat. At least she followed the other rules for eating lunch with the Queen, she thinks. Nobody ever said anything about vomiting.

SUMMARY

Ursula is a young girl. She lives in London, England. She is obsessed with the royal family. She eats dinner with her mother and watches TV. On TV, they announce a contest. The winner gets to eat lunch with the Queen herself. Ursula enters. The next day, at breakfast, they announce the winner. It is Ursula! She goes to Buckingham Palace for lunch. She follows the rules for eating with the Queen. The Queen has prepared special sandwiches. Unfortunately, leek salad is not Ursula's favorite food. She feels sick as she watches the Queen eat the sandwich.

Lista de Vocabulario

is	es / está
has	ha / has
to be	ser / estar
have	tener
are	eres / estás
leeks	puerros
am	soy / estoy
vegetable	vegetales
carrot	zanahoria
broccoli	brócoli
salad	ensalada
lunch	almuerzo

have to	tener que
dessert	postre
grapes	uvas
cherries	cerezas
fruit	fruta
cream	crema
sugar	azúcar
meal	comida
breakfast	desayuno
cereal	cereal
egg	huevo
bacon	tocino
sandwiches	sándwiches
tea	té
ham	jamón

cheese	queso
mustard	mostaza
cookies	galletas
scones	bollos
salad	ensalada

QUESTIONS

1) What happens when Ursula tries leeks for the first time?

      a) she loves them

      b) her mother burns them

      c) she almost vomits

      d) she doesn't notice

2) Which is a rule when you eat with the Queen of England?

      a) you must not eat until she eats

      b) you must wear blue

      c) you must eat sandwiches

      d) you must sit before she does

3) What does Ursula's mom think about the contest?

 a) Ursula has a chance to win

 b) it is fake

 c) the Queen should not be involved

 d) Ursula will never win

4) What does the Queen have for lunch?

 a) a good roast

 b) salmon, her favorite

 c) tea cookies and sandwiches

 d) it's top secret

5) Which of the following statements is true?

 a) Ursula leaves in the middle of lunch

 b) Ursula can't control her reaction to leeks

 c) the Queen made the sandwiches herself

 d) sandwiches are not good lunch food

ANSWERS

1) What happens when Ursula tries leeks for the first time?

      c) she almost vomits

2) Which is a rule when you eat with the Queen of England?

      a) you must not eat until she eats

3) What does Ursula's mom think about the contest?

      d) Ursula will never win

4) What does the Queen have for lunch?

      c) tea cookies and sandwiches

5) Which of the following statements is true?

      b) Ursula can't control her reaction to leeks

CAPÍTULO 10: Licencia de Conducir / Preguntas - The Driver's License / question words

STORY

Wayne lives in a city. Wayne is forty years old. He usually drives his car to work. Wayne is late to work today. Wayne drives faster and faster. He drives over the speed limit. He needs to get to work on time. Today he has an important meeting.

Wayne hears a sound. He looks behind him. There is a police car behind him. Oh, no, he thinks. I am going rather fast. He stops the car. The police car stops, too. A policeman gets out. He walks over to Wayne's car.

"Hello," says the police officer.

"Hello, sir," says Wayne.

"**Why** do you think I pulled you over?" asks the policeman.

"I don't know. **Which** law am I breaking?" asks Wayne.

"You are going way too fast," says the policeman.

"**How many** kilometers per hour am I over the speed limit?" asks Wayne.

"Enough," says the policeman. "**Where** are you going in such a hurry?"

"To work," says Wayne.

"Show me your driver's license," says the officer. Wayne takes out his wallet. He opens it. He pulls out his driver's license. He gives it to the police officer.

"This is expired," says the officer. "You're in big trouble." The officer tells Wayne he can't drive with an expired license. Wayne must get a new license. Wayne agrees. The officer tells him he can't drive to work today. Wayne must live without a car.

Wayne has to stop driving his car. Now he goes to work other ways. He can choose between the train or the bus. Sometimes, he rides his bike. If he is late, he takes a taxi. Today, he is late again.

Wayne arrives to the office.

"Hi, Wayne," says his colleague, Xavier. "**How** did you get here? Your license is expired, right?"

"Yes, it is," says Wayne. "Today I am in taxi. **How far** is your house from here?" Xavier usually walks to work.

"My house is a kilometer away," says Xavier. "**How long** does a taxi take to get here?"
"Oh, about twenty minutes," says Wayne.

"Not bad," says Xavier. "And **how much** does the taxi cost?"

"About twenty dollars," says Wayne.

"Oh, that is a bit expensive," says Xavier. "Which taxi company is it?

"Birmingham Taxi," says Wayne. "Why are you so interested?"

"My family owns a taxi company," says Xavier. "My brother runs it."

"Nice," says Wayne. "Can I get a free ride?" They both laugh. Wayne is kidding. But he needs to solve his problem. He can't pay for a taxi every day. He decides tomorrow he is going to get his license.

The next day, Wayne takes the bus to the DMV, the Department of Motor Vehicles. This is the building where people get their driver's license. He gets out of his car. There is a line outside. Many people have to get their license. The office is slow. He gets in the line. After an hour, he is inside the building. There is another line. He waits.

"**Who** is next?" asks the woman.

"Me," says Wayne.

"Well, come on!" she says. She is impatient. "**What** do you need?"

"I need to renew my license," says Wayne.

"Give me your old card," she says.

"I don't have it," says Wayne. She stares at him. She seems angry.

"**Why don't** you have it?" she asks.

"I can't find it," says Wayne.

"**With whom** am I speaking?" she asks.

"What do you mean?" asks Wayne. He is confused.

"Ok, smart guy, tell me your first and last name," she says. Wayne tells her.

"**How old** are you?" she asks.

"**What for**?" asks Wayne.

"I have to confirm your birth date," she says. "**When were you born?**"

Wayne tells her. She looks at her computer. She takes a long time. She shakes her head.

"I can't find you," she says. "There is a problem with the system today. Come back tomorrow."

"I can't," says Wayne.

"If you want your license today, you will have to take the driving test over," she says.

"**How come**?" asks Wayne.

"The computer says you have no license," she says. Wayne needs his license today. He goes to the other line. He will take his driver's test. Easy, he thinks. He knows how to drive. All the other people are teenagers. He is the oldest in this line.

"**Whose** turn is it?" asks a big man with a brown suit.

"Mine," says Wayne. He follows the big man to his car. They get in the car. Wayne tries to remember everything you do in a driver's test. He checks the mirrors. He puts on his seatbelt. He sees the examiner writing on a notepad.

"Okay, let's go," says the examiner.

Wayne carefully backs out of the parking space. He drives slowly. He uses his turn signal. He gets on the road and drives under the speed limit. The examiner directs him through the town. Wayne makes sure to stop at yellow lights and to use his blinker. Wayne does a good job.

Wayne thinks he passes. The examiner directs him back to the DMV. However, the examiner tells him to stop.

"Now you must parallel park," says the examiner. Wayne never parallel parks. He is nervous. The examiner directs him to a tiny parking space. Wayne turns the car into the space. He is almost finished parking. But then he hears a 'ding' sound. His car hits the car behind him.

"Oh, no," says Wayne.

"That is an automatic fail," says the examiner. "Sorry, you fail your driver's test."

Wayne gets out of the car to let the examiner drive the car back to the office.

"How many years have you been driving?" asks the examiner.

"Twenty-four," says Wayne. He is ashamed. He has to come back tomorrow.

SUMMARY

Wayne has a driver's license. It is expired. Wayne must take taxis, buses and other forms of transport. He decides to renew his license. He goes to the DMV to do it. He waits in a long line and has to answer a lot of questions. There is a problem with the computer system. Wayne has to take the driving test again from zero. He does a good job with the examiner in the car. However, Wayne fails his test because he hasn't practiced parallel parking.

Lista de Vocabulario

why	por qué
which	cual
how many	cuántos
where	donde
how	cómo
how far	hasta dónde
how long	cuánto tiempo
how much	cuánto
who	quién
what	qué

why don't	por qué no
with whom	con quien
how old	cuántos años
what for	qué para
when	cuando
how come	cómo es que
whose	de quién
how many	cuántos

QUESTIONS

1) Why does Wayne get stopped by the police officer?

    a) he runs a red light

    b) his car is broken

    c) he is going too fast

    d) he is a criminal

2) Wayne gets in big trouble with the officer because...

    a) his license is expired

    b) his car is not registered

c) he spits at the police officer

d) he does not answer the police officer

3) Which of these costs $20 for Wayne to use to get to work?

    a) bike

    b) bus

    c) train

    d) taxi

4) Wayne does not show up in the computer system at the DMV. Why?

    a) he never had a license

    b) he has a bad day

    c) there is a problem with the system

    d) his birthday is wrong

5) Why does Wayne fail his test?

    a) he is new at driving

    b) he parks badly because he hasn't practiced this type of parking

    c) he parks badly because the car is too big

    d) he is drunk

ANSWERS

1) Why does Wayne get stopped by the police officer?

    c) he is going too fast

2) Wayne gets in big trouble with the officer because...

    a) his license is expired

3) Which of these costs $20 for Wayne to use to get to work?

    d) taxi

4) Wayne does not show up in the computer system at the DMV. Why?

    c) there is a problem with the system

5) Why does Wayne fail his test?

    b) he parks badly because he hasn't practiced this type of parking

CAPÍTULO 11: En la Agencia de Viajes / Gustos y Disgustos - At The Travel Agency / likes and dislikes

STORY

Yolanda and Zelda are sisters. They have very busy lives. They both live in New York City. Yolanda is a hairdresser for celebrities. Zelda is a lawyer and has two children. They are so busy, sometimes they don't see each other for months.

Yolanda has an idea one day. She calls Zelda.

"Zelda, dear! How are you?" she asks.

"Fine, sis," says Zelda. "How are you?"

"Great! I've had a marvelous idea," says Yolanda. "**We should** take a trip together!"

"What a great idea," says Zelda. "**I love** it! Where to?"

"I don't know, anywhere," says Yolanda. "Wherever! **I would love** to go anywhere with you!"

"Let's go to the travel agency tomorrow," says Zelda. "They can help."

The sisters meet the next day. Zelda brings pages of research on vacations. The pages talk about different types of tourism. There is recreational tourism, like relaxing and having fun at the beach. There's cultural tourism like sightseeing or visiting museums to learn about history and art. Adventure tourism is for people who **adore** exploring distant places and extreme activities. Ecotourism is traveling to natural environments.

Yolanda reads the papers. Health tourism is travel to look after your body and mind by visiting places like spa resorts. Religious tourism is travel to celebrate religious events or visit important religious places.

"There are so many types of travel," says Yolanda.

"Yes," says Zelda. "**I enjoy** traveling for a reason. I can't stand lying on the beach, doing nothing." Yolanda likes the beach. She likes doing nothing on vacation. She doesn't say anything.

The sisters arrive to the travel agency. The travel agent is a woman. She seems nice. Yolanda and Zelda sit down with her.

"How can I help you?" asks the agent.

"We would like to take a trip," says Yolanda.

"What kind of trip?" asks the agent.

"**I'm crazy about** culture," says Zelda. "I love museums. I love art."

"**I would rather** go somewhere with sunshine. I love outdoor activities," says Yolanda.

"People travel for lots of reasons," says the agent. "How about Barcelona?"

"Oh, I don't know," says Zelda. "**I can't bear** not knowing the local language."

"We don't speak Spanish," says Yolanda.

"Would you like Paris?" asks the agent. "There are very good museums and restaurants."

"We don't speak French, either!" they both say.

"How about London?" asks the agent.

"Great!" says Zelda.

"So rainy!" says Yolanda at the same time. The sisters look at each other.

"You said you don't care Yoli!" says Zelda.

"I want to travel with you," says Yolanda. "**I'm not mad about** London, though. **I detest** the rain!"

"Come on, Yolanda," says Zelda. "Please!"

The agent shows the women pictures of London. They see the famous buildings. Yolanda would like to see Big Ben. Zelda is excited about the Tate Modern art museum.

"What kind of hotel would you like?" asks the agent.

"We could get an Airbnb apartment," says Yolanda.

"No, **I loathe** staying in other people's homes," says Zelda.

"We have beautiful hotels in the center of the city," says the agent.

"That sounds great," says Zelda.

Zelda prefers luxurious hotels. She knows Yolanda **doesn't like** fancy hotels **very much**. But Zelda never goes on vacation. She wants this vacation to be perfect. The travel agent shows the sisters pictures. The hotel rooms are huge. Some have a bath in the middle of the room.

"Those are gorgeous," says Zelda. "Do you mind if we stay in a fancy hotel, Yolanda?"

"**Not at all**," says Yolanda. Zelda knows she **dislikes** fancy hotels. Yolanda feels sad. Zelda does what she wants.

"What would you like to do while in London?" asks the travel agent.

"We would love to go to all the museums, visit the Palace, and visit some art galleries," says Zelda.

"Okay," says the travel agent. "That's probably enough to fill your time in London."

Yolanda doesn't say anything. The sisters pay and leave the travel agent. Zelda is happy. Yolanda wishes the vacation was more her style. She goes home. She thinks about the trip. She smiles. She has a plan.

The next day, Yolanda returns to the travel agent.

"Oh hello, Yolanda," says the agent. "How can I help you?"

"**We want** to change our trip a bit," says Yolanda.

"No problem," says the travel agent.

"**We would rather** go to somewhere sunny," says Yolanda.

"Of course," says the travel agent. The travel agent suggests many different locations. Yolanda signs some new papers. She gives the agent money for the change. She imagines Zelda on vacation. She smiles. Zelda **likes** surprises.

It is the weekend. It is time for Yolanda and Zelda's trip. The sisters meet at the airport. They are excited. Yolanda is nervous.

"I brought you coffee," she says. Zelda takes the coffee.

"Thanks," she says. She takes a sip. "Oh, but **I hate** sugar in my coffee, Yoli!"

Yolanda apologizes. She takes both coffees in her hands. Now she can't carry her suitcase.

The two sisters go through security. They wait to board the plane. The screen says "Flight 361 to London / With Connections / British Airways". Yolanda smiles as they get on the plane.

The flight lasts six hours. Yolanda and Zelda sleep. They awake as the plane pulls into the airport in London. The flight attendant uses the speaker. "If you are staying in London or have a connection, please stand and leave the plane."

Zelda stands up. Yolanda does not.

"Come on, Yolanda," says Zelda. Yolanda doesn't move.

"Let's go!" says Zelda.

"Actually, sis," says Yolanda. "There is a change of plans. We are staying on this plane."

Zelda looks confused.

The flight attendant uses the speaker again. "If you are traveling through to our next destination, remain in your seats. Next stop—Fiji!"

SUMMARY
Two sisters, Yolanda and Zelda, want to have a trip together. They go to the travel agent. They are very different. It is difficult for them to agree on a location. Zelda likes to plan vacations and see art and culture. Yolanda prefer Finally, they decide where they would like to go. But the next day, Yolanda returns to the travel agent. She changes the destination. Zelda finds out when their plane lands.

Lista de Vocabulario

we should	deberíamos
I love	Me encanta
I would love	Me encantaría
I adore	Yo adoro

I enjoy	Disfruto
I can't stand	No puedo estar de pie
we would like	nos gustaría
I'm crazy about	Estoy loco por
I prefer	Prefiero
I can't bear	No lo puedo soportar
would you like	te gustaría
I'm not mad about	No estoy enojado por
I detest	Detesto
I loathe	Odio
doesn't like	no le gusta
very much	mucho
not at all	para nada
dislikes	disgustos
what would you like	¿qué te gustaría

we want	queremos
we would rather	preferiríamos
likes	gustar
I hate	Yo odio

QUESTIONS

1) How do Yolanda and Zelda know each other?

    a) they are friends

    b) they are sisters

    c) they work together

    d) they are neighbors

2) What does Zelda like to do on vacation?

    a) see art and culture

    b) lay on the beach

    c) relax

    d) see what happens without plans

3) Which of the following does Yolanda decide at the first meeting with the travel agent?

a) where to go

b) where to stay

c) what to do

d) none of the above

4) What does Yolanda do when she goes to the travel agent the second time?

    a) asks for her money back

    b) cancels the trip

    c) changes the destination

    d) calls Zelda

5) What happens when the sisters land in London?

    a) they go to their hotel

    b) they go to a museum

    c) the plane crashes

    d) Yolanda surprises Zelda with a new destination

ANSWERS

1) How do Yolanda and Zelda know each other?

    b) they are sisters

2) What does Zelda like to do on vacation?

a) see art and culture

3) Which of the following does Yolanda decide at the first meeting with the travel agent?

d) none of the above

4) What does Yolanda do when she goes to the travel agent the second time?

c) changes the destination

5) What happens when the sisters land in London?

d) Yolanda surprises Zelda with a new destination

CAPÍTULO 12: San Valentín en París / Preposiciones - Valentine's Day in Paris / prepositions

STORY

Charles and Dana are boyfriend and girlfriend. They are in love. Charles wants to do something special for Valentine's Day. He invites Dana to Paris. Paris is called the city of love. Many people travel to Paris to spend romantic time with their partner. Maybe it is the movies, the food, the beautiful buildings? Paris always feels romantic.

The couple arrives to Paris on February 13. The plane lands. They are thrilled. Charles and Dana collect their baggage.

"Let's go to the hotel," says Charles.

"How?" asks Dana.

"We can take the train to the city center," says Charles. **In front of** the couple is a sign for the airport train. They follow the arrows, walking **beneath** them. They walk **across** the sky bridge, until they come to the entrance to the train. They go up to the ticket machine.

"Which ticket do we buy?" asks Dana. They both stare at the machine.

"I don't know," says Charles. "The hotel is **in** the 7th arrondissement." Charles guesses which ticket to buy. He buys it and they go to the train platform. **Above** the tracks, there is a sign. It tells where each train is going. A train approaches. The sign says 'centre-ville'. They get **into** the train.

When the train reaches the destination, they get **off** the train. They go up the metro stairs. They step outside. The Eiffel Tower stands **above** them.

"It's beautiful," says Dana.

"Yes, it's amazing," says Charles.

"I want to go **to** the top," says Dana.

"Did you know they paint the tower every seven years?" asks Charles. "With 50 tons of paint!"

"I didn't know that," says Dana. Charles tells her more about the Eiffel Tower. It was built in 1889. It is named after Gustave Eiffel, the architect in charge of the project. For 41 years, it was the tallest structure in the world. There are many replicas of the tower **around** the world. There is even a full-size replica in Tokyo.

"I love Paris," says Dana.

"Let's go to the hotel," says Charles. They walk to the nearby hotel. It is just **behind** the Eiffel Tower.

The next day is Valentine's Day. The couple has a special lunch planned. They go to the restaurant Epicure. It is one of the city's most romantic restaurants.

"Are you ready?" asks Charles.

"Yes," says Dana. "How do we get there?" They walk **out of** the hotel.

"It is just **past** the Champs-Élysées," says Charles. They walk **down** the street. They walk **toward** the river. It is a beautiful day. The sun is shining. Dana notices how beautiful the buildings are. They are all very old.

"We should have buildings like this in America," says Dana.

"They are older than America," says Charles. Charles and Dana walk **along** the river. They hold hands. Paris is a city for lovers.

Epicure is **near** the central shopping district. They pass shops like Louis Vuitton and Pierre Hermé. Dana stops to look in the windows. The restaurant is **next to** one of her favorite shops.

"Please can we go in," she says. When they go **through** the door of Hermes, Charles knows he is in trouble. Purses and scarves are everywhere. Dana goes crazy.

She takes two scarves **from** a display. She grabs a bag from **amongst** a pile of purses.

"Please, Charles?" she asks him. "A little Paris souvenir?" Charles thinks. The three items cost the same as the airplane ticket to Paris. It is Valentine's Day, though. He says yes. Dana takes the scarves and the purse to the cash register. Charles pays with his credit card. They leave the shop. Dana is very content.

Charles and Dana continue down the street. They don't see Epicure.

"It is right here," says Charles.

"Right where?" asks Dana.

"Here," says Charles. "That is what Google maps says."

"I don't see it," says Dana.

Charles calls the restaurant on his cell phone. "Hello, we cannot find the restaurant," he says. He listens. The person speaks French. "Do you speak English? No?" The person hangs up.

"They don't speak English," says Charles.

"It has to be here," says Dana. She spots a small alley. She enters the alleyway and walks a bit.

"Here it is," she says. The restaurant is **within** the alleyway, hidden **at** the very end.

"Thank goodness," says Charles. "We are already late!" They enter the restaurant.

"Do you have a reservation?" asks the waiter.

"Yes," says Charles. "We are a bit late. Charles."

"Follow me," says the waiter. They follow the waiter. They walk between tables with white tablecloths. They are the first diners. The restaurant is empty.

"It's beautiful," says Dana. They sit at their table. It has fresh flowers **on** it. Their table is **beside** the fire. A golden chandelier hangs from the ceiling.

"What would you like?" asks the waiter.

"The chicken with mushrooms, and the macaroni with foie gras and artichoke," says Charles.

"I recommend the macaroni **before** the chicken," says the waiter.

"Ok," says Charles.

"The chicken is served with a side salad," says the waiter.

"Perfect," says Charles. "And please bring us some champagne." Charles winks at the waiter.

"Why did you wink at him?" asks Dana.

"I didn't mean to!" says Charles.

Dana and Charles are very happy. The restaurant is one of the best in Paris. It has three Michelin stars. The waiter comes up **behind** Charles with the macaroni. It is very rich. It has black truffle on top. They agree, it is the best macaroni they have ever had.

The waiter rolls a cart to the table. It has two glasses, a bottle of champagne, and a black box. The waiter opens the wine and pours it for Charles and Dana. He leaves the black box on the table.

"What's that?" asks Dana.

"Dana, will you marry me?" asks Charles. He lifts the top of the black box. **Below** is a huge diamond ring. He puts it on Dana's finger.

"Yes!" shouts Dana.

Paris really is the city of love.

SUMMARY
Charles and Dana are in love. They take a trip to Paris for Valentine's Day. They get lost looking for their

hotel. They don't understand the metro. Neither Charles nor Dana speaks French. Charles reserves a special lunch for Valentine's Day. Dana can't resist the shops of Paris. They have a hard time finding the restaurant. Dana finds the restaurant down an alley. At lunch, Charles has a secret surprise for Dana. What is it? A token of true love. A waiter at the restaurant brings the ring with the champagne. Charles asks Dana to marry him.

Lista de Vocabulario

in front of	delante de
beneath	debajo
across	a través de
in	en
above	encima de
into	en
off	fuera
above	más arriba

to	a
around	alrededor
behind	detrás
out of	fuera de
past	pasado
down	abajo
toward	hacia
along	a lo largo
near	cerca
next to	al lado de
through	a través
from	desde
amongst	entre
within	dentro de
at	en

between	entre
on	en
beside	al lado
before	antes de
with	con
behind	detrás
below	debajo

QUESTIONS

1) Who had the idea to go on the vacation to Paris?

    a) Charles

    b) the father of Charles

    c) the travel agent

    d) Dana

2) What is the first thing Charles and Dana see in Paris?

    a) the Louvre

    b) the Champs-Élysées

c) the hotel

d) the Eiffel Tower

3) What other city in the world has a full-size Eiffel Tower?

    a) New York

    b) Tokyo

    c) Dubai

    d) Hong Kong

4) What does Dana convince Charles to do on Valentine's Day?

    a) go home

    b) go to the museum

    c) buy her something at Hermes

    d) stop drinking

5) How does Charles give Dana the engagement ring?

    a) a waiter brings it out with the champagne

    b) he puts it in her ice cream

    c) he takes it from his pocket

    d) he gets on his knees

ANSWERS

1) Who had the idea to go on the vacation to Paris?

    a) Charles

2) What is the first thing Charles and Dana see in Paris?

    d) the Eiffel Tower

3) What other city in the world has a full-size Eiffel Tower?

    b) Tokyo

4) What does Dana convince Charles to do on Valentine's Day?

    c) buy her something at Hermes

5) How does Charles give Dana the engagement ring?

    a) a waiter brings it out with the champagne

CAPÍTULO 13: Nuevas Compañeras de Cuarto/Objetos Comunes de la Vida Cotidiana y Posesiones - New Roommates/Common everyday objects + possession

STORY

Today is move-in day at the university. First year students move **their** things into the dormitory.

Anna arrives to the university with her parents. **Her** car is loaded with **boxes**. Anna brings everything she needs for a year of school with her. They park outside of Anna's dormitory. The building is a big, brick building. It looks boring. Anna tries to think positive. This year will be great, she tells herself.

Her family begins to unload the car. Anna is very prepared. They take out boxes full of her things. Her brother helps her take the boxes up to the room. The room is small. There are two beds. Anna will have a roommate.

The first box Anna opens has school supplies. She puts her **notepads**, **pencils** and **pens** on her desk. The room has no decoration, except for a **television** on the wall. Anna organizes her things in the room. She takes her **calendar** out to put on the wall.

"This isn't **mine**!" she says. It is a calendar of pretty women.

"This is **his**," Anna says, pointing at her brother.
"Oh, sorry," says her brother. Anna throws it in the **trash can**. The family laughs.

There is a knock on the door. They open the door. A blonde girl stands outside. She is with an older woman, her mother.

"Hello, I'm Beatriz," says the girl.

"I'm Anna," says Anna. "I guess we are roommates!"

"Where are you from?" asks Beatriz.

"Nearby, just an hour north," says Anna.

"Me too!" says Beatriz.

The girls shake hands and smile. Beatriz brings her own boxes. The families help their daughters unpack.

The first days of school are nice. Anna makes new friends. She and Beatriz get along great. Anna goes to her new classes. Everything is perfect. However, one thing is wrong. Some of Anna's belongings begin to disappear. First, she can't find her **brush**. Then, the next day, she looks in the **mirror**. She sees her **lotion** but her **perfume** is missing. When she arrives from class that evening, she puts on some music. There is no sound. Her **speaker** is gone!
She asks Beatriz. "Beatriz," she says. "Are you missing anything?"

"Yes!" says Beatriz. "My laptop **computer**. I am freaking out."

"Oh no!" says Anna. "I am missing a few things, too."

Anna is missing three things now. She calls her mother on her **cell phone**.

"Hi, mom," says Anna.

"Hi, honey," says her mom. "How is school?"

"Fine," says Anna. "But my belongings keep disappearing."

"What do you mean?" asks her mom. Anna tells her mom about the missing perfume, the missing speaker, and the missing brush.

"That is so strange," says her mom. "Did you take them somewhere?"

"No, mom," says Anna. "I never left the room. The rest of the **stereo system** is here. My **mp3 player,** too."

"Do you lock your door?" asks her mom.

"Yes, mom!" says Anna. "And it's just the perfume that is gone. I still have all the other **makeup, lipstick**, everything!"

"Do you think it could be Beatriz?" asks her mom.

"No way, she is missing stuff too," says Anna.

"Ok, go check the lost-and-found," says Anna's mom.

"Ok! Gotta go," says Anna.

Anna hangs up the phone. Her mom's idea is good. She goes downstairs to the dormitory office. She asks to see the lost-and-found box. The box is full. She looks through it. She finds **notebooks**, a **video camera**, and even a **comb**. But does not see her things. She looks more. She sees a laptop **computer**.

"Is that **yours**?" she asks, thinking of Beatriz. She pulls it out. It is. She takes the computer to give to Beatriz. At least she finds something.

She goes upstairs. She gives Beatriz the computer.

"Wow, Anna, it's **my** computer!" says Beatriz. "Thank you so much."

"You're welcome," says Anna. "So glad I found **your** computer."
"Me too," says Beatriz. "Did you find any of your things?"

"No," says Anna.

"Bummer," says Beatriz. The girls go to sleep.

The next day, Beatriz has class. Anna stays in the dorm room. She works on a project, using **scissors** to cut pictures to glue on a **folder**. She thinks about her missing items. Maybe she should look in the dorm room. She looks everywhere. Then she turns to Beatriz's closet. She opens it. She looks inside it.

"This is mine!" says Anna. She pulls out her brush. She is shocked. Why is her brush in Beatriz's closet? She looks closer. Under a stack of **clothes**, she feels something hard. She pulls it out. It is her bottle of perfume! When she looks closer, she finds her speaker, too.

"It was Beatriz the whole time," says Anna. The room **telephone** rings. Anna answers. It is Beatriz's mom.

"Hi, Anna," says Beatriz's mom. "How are you?"

"Fine," says Anna. "Beatriz isn't here."

"Can you tell her I called?" asks Beatriz's mom.
"Yes, but, can I talk to you about something?" asks Anna.
"Sure," says Beatriz's mom.

"Some of my things have gone missing," says Anna. "And I just found many of them in **your** daughter's closet."

"Oh, no," says Beatriz's mom. "I need to tell you something."

"What?" says Anna.

"Beatriz is a kleptomaniac," says her mom. "She takes things and then returns them exactly seven days later. She will return those items to you by tomorrow."

"What do I do?" asks Anna.

"Just wait for her to return them," says her mom.

"Okay," says Anna.

"Thank you for understanding," says Beatriz's mom.

SUMMARY

Anna and Beatriz are roommates. It is their first year at university. They meet on move-in day. They get their dorm room set up. Their parents help. They get along well. During the first week, many of Anna's possessions go missing. She cannot find them anywhere. Beatriz also has some missing items. Anna looks everywhere. She looks in the lost and found, where she finds Beatriz's missing computer. When Beatriz isn't there, Anna looks in her closet. She finds all her items. Beatriz's mom calls. She tells Anna that Beatriz is a kleptomaniac.

Lista de Vocabulario

their	su (3ra persona)
her	su (femenino)
boxes	cajas
mine	mío
notepads	blocs de notas
pencils	lápices
pens	bolígrafos
television	televisión
calendar	calendario
his	su (masculino)
trash can	bote de basura
brush	cepillo
mirror	espejo
lotion	loción

perfume	perfume
speaker	altavoz
computer	computadora
cell phone	teléfono celular
stereo system	sistema estéreo
makeup	maquillaje
lipstick	pintalabios
notebook	cuaderno
video camera	cámara de vídeo
comb	peine
my	mi
yours	tus / sus
your	tu / su
scissors	tijeras
clothes	ropa

telephone	telefono
your	tu / su

QUESTIONS

1) How do Beatriz and Anna know each other?

    a) they have been friends forever

    b) they meet at class

    c) they are roommates

    d) they go to the same school

2) Which of these items did not go missing?

    a) brush

    b) perfume

    c) speaker

    d) mirror

3) What does Anna's mom suggest?

    a) that Anna come home

    b) that Anna confront Beatriz

    c) that Anna buy a new brush

d) that Anna look in the lost and found

4) What does Anna find in the lost and found?

    a) her brush

    b) Beatriz's computer

    c) a sweatshirt

    d) her perfume

5) What happened to Anna's things?

    a) Beatriz took them and put them in her closet

    b) Anna lost them

    c) Anna threw them away

    d) nothing

ANSWERS

1) How do Beatriz and Anna know each other?

    c) they are roommates

2) Which of these items did not go missing?

    d) mirror

3) What does Anna's mom suggest?

d) that Anna look in the lost and found

4) What does Anna find in the lost and found?

b) Beatriz's computer

5) What happened to Anna's things?

a) Beatriz took them and put them in her closet

CAPÍTULO 14: Un Día en la Vida / Palabras de Transición - A Day in the Life / transition words

STORY

Bey wakes up in a hotel room. She is tired. Her body is tired, **but** her mind is more tired. She feels alone. Her friends and family don't understand what it is like to be famous. She laughs. They want to be famous. They want to spend a day in her life. People think celebrities have fun all day. They think celebrities get anything they want. **However,** Bey knows this is not true.

Why do people want to be famous? Bey thinks. She makes a coffee. The media shows her as success. People want success. They want a perfect life. **As a result,** they try to become famous. She knows life is not perfect.

The clock says seven o'clock. Her day is busy. **Therefore**, she has to wake up early. Some people think celebrities sleep late. She has a lot to do. There is no time to sleep late. She hears the doorbell.

"Hello," says Bey.

"Hi, Bey," say the three women. One woman is her stylist. Another woman is her makeup artist. **Lastly**, the hairdresser enters. She opens the door. They go inside. They begin to work.

"Which shirt?" says the stylist.

"Which color of lipstick?" asks the makeup artist.

"Why did you sleep with your hair like that?" asks the hairdresser.

Bey's coffee is cold. She makes another coffee. **Then**, she answers all the questions. They help her. **Finally**, she is ready.

She leaves the hotel at 10 a.m. There are many people outside. They wait for her. When she goes out, they scream. They take pictures. Bey gets in a car. The car has dark windows. No one can see in. **Therefore,** she can do what she wants. She relaxes. Her phone rings.

"Hello?" she says.

"Bey, where are you?" asks her manager.

"In the car," she says.

"You're late!" says the manager.

"Sorry," said Bey. She has dance practice, voice lessons, and a photo shoot. A busy day. Her manager keeps her schedule. He tells her what to do. He tells her when to go. She feels stuck. She must work to stay famous. She can't take a vacation.

The car stops. **First**, Bey has a photo shoot. It is for a magazine. A girl puts makeup on Bey. She is a fan. She smiles.

"How are you?" she asks.

"Fine," says Bey.

"I am your fan," she says.

"Thank you," says Bey.

"I sing, too," the girl says. She powders Bey's face.

"Really?" asks Bey. She is bored.

"Yes. I want to be famous!" says the girl.

"Being famous is a lot of work!" says Bey.

"I don't care!" says the girl.

"What are you doing tonight?" asks Bey.
"Dinner with my boyfriend, a walk in the park, maybe visit a museum," says the girl.

"I have work, a concert," says Bey. "**In fact,** I have one every night. I can't go out to the park **because** people recognize me. They don't leave me alone."

"Oh," says the girl. She finishes the makeup.

"**For example**, I can't remember a visit to a museum," says Bey. She is finished. She takes her pictures. Her dress is glamorous. She looks beautiful and happy. She says goodbye and gets in the car.

Second, Bey has dance practice. She practices in a dance studio. Her teacher is professional. They practice for the concert. Tonight's concert is in a stadium in New York City. She forgets the dance for her most famous song. She practices for two hours. **Without a doubt**, she knows the dance.

Third, Bey has voice lessons. Famous singers need lessons. Voice lessons help them sing easily. This is important. **After all,** singing a concert every night is difficult.

After voice, she eats lunch. Her assistant brings it to her. Even though it is quick, it is healthy. She has a smoothie and a salad. Soon she must prepare for the concert.

She checks her phone. Bey has another assistant. This assistant does social media. She puts pictures on Instagram and Facebook. **Ultimately**, Bey likes to see for herself. Her new picture has 1,000,000 likes. Not bad, she thinks. It also has many comments. Some are mean, **so** Bey turns off her phone. She tries to be positive.

In the car, Bey calls her friends. She talks to her mother. She talks in the car **since** she doesn't have much time. She is tired. She has a headache. Maybe she can nap. She looks at her phone. It is too late to nap.

While Bey gets ready, fans wait. They make a line outside. They are excited. They paid a lot of money for the tickets.

Now her throat hurts. She drinks warm tea. **If** she can't sing, the fans will be sad. She looks at her phone. She has a picture saved for these moments. It is a letter.

"Dear Bey," it says.

"You are my favorite singer. I think you are amazing. I want to be just like you when I grow up. Love, Susy." It is from a 7-year-old fan. Bey remembers her. She smiles. There are hundreds of girls like Susy at the concert. **For this reason,** she performs.

Eventually, the concert ends.

More and more fans ask for Bey's autograph. They smile. They take pictures on their phone. She imagines their lives. They go to parties. They see friends. They go to restaurants. **Either way**, they have freedom. She is jealous. **Despite** not being famous, they have better lives.

She thinks of the makeup girl from today. She wonders, what is she doing now? Bey thinks maybe she will quit.

All of a sudden, her phone makes a sound.

It is a reminder to go to bed. Tomorrow is another busy day.

SUMMARY

Bey is a celebrity. She is a famous pop singer. People are jealous of her life. However, it is not easy. Her day begins early. Her three assistants come to the hotel. They get her ready. Then, she has a busy day. She goes to a photo shoot. The makeup girl wants to be famous. Bey says it is not that great. Bey practices dance and singing. Then she gets ready for her concert. She feels sick. However, she performs for her many fans. She takes pictures and signs autographs. She feels jealous of her fans' normal lives.

Lista de Vocabulario

but	pero
however	sin embargo
as a result	como resultado
therefore	por lo tanto
lastly	por último

then	entonces
finally	finalmente
therefore	por lo tanto
first	primero
in fact	de hecho
because	porque
for example	por ejemplo
second	segundo
without a doubt	sin duda
after all	después de todo
even though	aunque
ultimately	en última instancia
so	así que
since	desde que
while	mientras

if	si
for this reason	por esta razón
Eventually.	Eventualmente.
either way	de cualquier manera
despite	a pesar de
all of a sudden	de repente

QUESTIONS

1) Which person does not come to Bey's hotel?

    a) a makeup artist

    b) a stylist

    c) a fan

    d) a hairdresser

2) Why does Bey's manager call her?

    a) to ask where she is

    b) to fire her

    c) to congratulate her

d) to ask how she is

3) What is Bey's job?

 a) a dancer

 b) a pop star

 c) a talk show host

 d) a photographer

4) What does Bey do to help her sing?

 a) she drinks tea

 b) she goes to voice lessons

 c) she prays

 d) she crosses her fingers

5) What does the sound from the phone mean at the end of the story?

 a) someone is calling

 b) it's time to take medicine

 c) a notification from Instagram

 d) it's time to go to bed

ANSWERS

1) Which person does not come to Bey's hotel?

    c) a fan

2) Why does Bey's manager call her?

    a) to ask where she is

3) What is Bey's job?

    b) a pop star

4) What does Bey do to help her sing?

    b) she goes to voice lessons

5) What does the sound from the phone mean at the end of the story?

    d) it's time to go to bed

CAPÍTULO 15: El Camino Inspiración / Números y Familia - The Camino Inspiration / Numbers + Family

Molly loves adventures.

She is the bravest member of her **family**, even braver than her **two brothers**. She often goes camping with her family in the woods. This weekend, they go to the mountain together. The moon shines and the birds and animals are quiet. Molly sits with her brothers and her **sister** by the fire, talking and playing. They see a bat fly over their heads.

"Ewww!" shouts Molly's sister.

"A bat!" yells **one** of Molly's brothers.

Then, **three** more bats fly over their heads.

"Ahhh! Let's get **mom** and **dad**!" shouts the other brother, John.

"It's only a bat," says Molly.

More bats arrive, until there are **eight** flying overhead. Molly's sister and brothers disappear into their tents, scared out of their wits. Molly does not move. She watches as the bats circled, now **nineteen**, no, **twenty**!

"Hi, Molly," says her **mother**, walking up behind her **father** to the campfire.

"Wow, there sure are a lot of bats around these woods," says her dad. "Aren't you scared?"

Molly shook her head no, and watched the bats fly off into the starry night sky.

"Let's eat dinner!" she said. Her brothers and sister come out of their tents. The family eats by the fire. They love to camp together.

Molly is **twenty-two**. She just graduated from college, where she studied engineering. She has not found a job in an office, so she works at her local outdoor store. She saves her paycheck and gets to talk about her favorite hobby all day: camping.

Every Saturday, Molly works on the **second** floor, with all of the tents, backpacks, and camping supplies. This Saturday, in walks her **cousin**.

"Hi, Jim!" says Molly, a happy smile on her face.

"Molly! I forgot you work here," says Jim, the **thirty-**year-old **son** of Molly's **aunt** Jane.

"How are Aunt Jane and **Uncle** Joe?" asks Molly.

"They're good. This weekend they are visiting **Grandma** Gloria at her house," says Jim. "I'm here to buy some outdoor goods for a trip."

"Oh, sure! I can help you. What is on your list?" Molly asks.

Jim shows Molly a piece of paper with a list of **fifteen** items. A light backpack, a portable stove, **four** pairs of warm socks, hiking poles, Dr. Bronner's magic soap, a pocket knife, and **eighteen** dehydrated trail meals.

Wow, this sounds like quite a trip, thinks Molly.

"Gimme the lightest backpack you have," says Jim. "The lightest everything, actually. I have to keep my pack under **twenty-eight** pounds."

"What are you buying all of this for?" asks Molly, walking with Jim over to a wall filled with backpacks of all colors, large and small.

"I'm going to hike," says Jim. "Across Spain."

Jim tries on the different backpacks. He chooses Molly's favorite, a red backpack with **seven** pockets, four on the back and three inside. The pack is so light, it hardly weighs **two-and-a-half** pounds. He wears it on his shoulders as he follows Molly to the clothing section.

"It's called the Camino de Santiago," Jim tells Molly. Her cousin tells her about the hike. It is a pilgrimage to the Cathedral of Santiago de Compostela in Galicia. People say that Saint James is buried in the church.

Uncle Jim will be walking the hike from the common starting point of the French Way, Saint-Jean-Pied-de-Port. From there, it is about **five hundred** miles to Santiago. The pilgrimage has been popular since the Middle Ages. Criminals and other people walked the way in exchange for blessings. Nowadays, most travel by foot. Some people travel by bicycle. A few pilgrims even travel on a horse or donkey. The pilgrimage was religious, but now many do it for travel or sport.

"I need to travel," says Jim. "I need time to think and reflect. Walking 500 miles can be very spiritual."

Molly helps Jim find a waterproof jacket and a pair of pants that can unzip to be shorts. He seems very happy with his large bag of things. He has much more in his hands than the other shoppers. He is going on a real trip.

"That will be **three hundred forty-seven** dollars and **sixty-six** cents," says Molly.

"Thanks, Molly," says Jim.

Molly begins to think. She lives at home with her **parents**. Her mother works as a judge in the local courthouse and her father is a lawyer. They are both rarely home for dinner. They stay busy at the office until late. Her **siblings** live with their families in Seattle, three hours away. She is alone, with no real job. She has no one to stop her.

It will be the perfect vacation. And maybe she will decide what to do with the rest of her life.

Why not?

That day, Mollly decides that she will do the Camino de Santiago. Starting in September, three months from now. Alone.

SUMMARY

A young woman named Molly loves the outdoors. She and her family camp together often. She works at an outdoors store as she looks for a job after university. Her Uncle Jim visits to prepare for a trip. He is going to hike the Camino de Santiago and needs supplies. Molly helps him buy a backpack, shoes, and everything else he needs. She decides to go on the Camino herself.

Lista de Vocabulario

family	familia
two	dos
brother	hermano
sister	hermana
one	una
three	tres
mom	mamá
dad	papá
eight	ocho

nineteen	diecinueve
twenty	veinte
mother	madre
father	padre
twenty-two	veintidós
second	segundo
cousin	primo
thirty	treinta
son	hijo
aunt	tía
uncle	tío
grandma	abuela
fifteen	quince
four	cuatro
eighteen	dieciocho

twenty-eight	veintiocho
seven	siete
two-and-a-half	dos y medio
five hundred	quinientos
three hundred	trescientos
forty-seven	cuarenta y siete
sixty-six	sesenta y seis
parents	padres
siblings	hermanos

QUESTIONS

1) What did Molly study at university?

    a) cosmetology

    b) literature

    c) engineering

    d) marketing

2) How many siblings does Molly have?

a) one

b) two

c) three

d) four

3) How is Jim related to Molly?

    a) brother

    b) uncle

    c) grandfather

    d) dad

4) What is the Camino de Santiago?

    a) a pilgrimage

    b) a city

    c) a church

    d) a holiday

5) Where is Molly from?

    a) the United States

    b) England

    c) Australia

    d) France

ANSWERS

1) What did Molly study at university?

    c) engineering

2) How many siblings does Molly have?

    c) three

3) How is Jim related to Molly?

    b) uncle

4) What is the Camino de Santiago?

    a) a pilgrimage

5) Where is Molly from?

    a) the United States

CPSIA information can be obtained
at www.ICGtesting.com
Printed in the USA
BVHW031011150321
602551BV00004B/217

9 781913 907877